COACHING
LEADERS

Leverage the Power of Your Inner
Voices to Become a Leader

Laura Fierro Evans

ISBN: 978-1-3123-4771-7 (sc)
ISBN: 978-1-4834-2812-3 (e)

Library of Congress Control Number: 2015904074

Lulu Publishing Services rev. date: 3/30/2015

To my parents, Manuel and Mary, whose voices
have lived within me forever.
To Alex and Damian, because through my voice,
they heard the echo of their grandparents' voices.
To Paola, Andrea, and Gabriel, who hear
through their parents' voices the echo
and vibration of the cultures
before them.

I live in a world of others' words. And my entire life is an orientation in this world, a reaction to other's words, beginning with my assimilation of them and ending with assimilation of the wealth of human culture.

—Mikhail Bakhtin

Contents

Preface

Coaching, as understood in the International Coaching Federation, is a process that enhances awareness in the one being coached. By stimulating his creative thought process, he can further develop his potential and overcome his obstacles to progress.

Through a semistructured conversation, a coach supports the client's cognitive and creative process. Using highly developed listening skills, he asks thought-provoking questions that serve to broaden the client's point of view and push the limits of his awareness. The conversation ends when the client himself identifies new behaviors that can help him reach his goals and become ready to focus on integrating them into his daily life.

Coaching works on at least two levels. On the transactional level, these goals bring an improvement in personal efficiency, and on the development level, it teaches the coachee new ways of thinking when facing his own challenges. However, there is a third level on which coaching can also work, which we call the transformational level. Here, the client redefines the way he assigns meaning to, or "knows" himself, his own identity, and the circumstances around him. Robert Kegan, a professor at Harvard University, indicates that transformative learning occurs when a person changes not just his behavior, not just his perception of reality, but also the way he learns. So, it's not only about *what* a person learns, but *how*.

"New information can be added to things that are already known by an individual, but transformation changes the way in which said person gets to know such things."[1]

After many years of work in the world of personal and collective

---

[1] Kegan, *In Over Our Heads: The Mental Demands of Modern Life.*

transformation, I have been constructing an increasingly precise idea as to identifying what produces a transformational intervention and the elements that make it so. My experience has led me to identify three fundamental aspects in the transformation processes.

1. Separating the coachee from how he identifies himself. The coachee is "subject" to his own emotions, convictions, mind-set, personality, and behavior, which remain invisible and unconscious, in the sense that he cannot separate them from himself. As such, the coachee can't evaluate himself, nor can he observe or reflect upon these parts to which he is "subject." To counter this, the coaching process enables the coachee to move these elements to which he has been "subject," to an "object" position, different and separate from himself—at which point he is able to observe, appraise, question, and modify these parts of his personality and become fully responsible for them.

2. Becoming fully aware that every irritation comes from disowned parts of the personality that have been projected. Assuming full responsibility for his emotions, beliefs, mind-set, personality, and the dominant—or "primary" behavior, to use the language of voice dialogue—involves the coachee becoming aware that every irritation, every time someone does something that "presses his buttons," he experiences a reaction that is nothing more than the projection of a part of himself that he has not accepted: his "shadow" part. Developing this awareness allows the coachee to make conscious decisions and to stay at a "choosing point" instead of unconsciously letting himself be governed by emotions, fears, and habits, and so remain the victim of others or circumstances.

3. Integration of "polarities." When the coachee is successful in separating from those portions of himself that govern his behavior, he starts observing, appraising, and integrating the polar opposites that are his projections or "shadow" parts. This marks the beginning of a restructuring process of the ego in a way that expands, evolves, and transforms. The coachee no longer identifies himself

with this or that emotion, behavior, or mind-set. Instead of embracing a single pole, he develops the ability to feel at ease between the opposites. This is how the coachee becomes empowered and able to trust himself in any situation, especially those in which ambiguity and uncertainty prevail. This skill is essential to being able to face the challenges of a time marked by unprecedented change.

The inner team model described by Laura contains the essentials of powerful transformational work because it combines these three elements. The model stems from the work of Hal and Sidra Stone, who have, from the seventies, developed what we know as the "Psychology of Selves." This method invites us to view "I" and "me" not as a coherent entity but as a combination of different "individuals" (or different voices), which come together as "I."

As anyone knows when making an important decision, "I" becomes a confusing struggle for recognition by various personalities that live within, each with their conflicting points of view, needs, and aspirations.

Inner team dialogue offers a way of communicating and working with the various "individuals" within a client. Coaching facilitates an exchange between members of the inner team, which brings about powerful shifts in consciousness that lead beyond the learning process to transformation.

This book is written in simple terms with an easy narrative style. Laura has added huge value and impact to the coaching world by bringing us the inner team model.

Giovanna D'Alessio, MCC
President of ICF International for 2010 and 2011

Acknowledgments

I thank each of the many clients who have inspired this work. The character that I call Miguel represents the echoes of several voices drawn from memory. The name of the character, Miguel Antonio Hernández López, is fictional, as are the locations, the company for which he works, and the story itself. Should there be any similarity with people or facts that exist in reality, this would be entirely a coincidence.

My special gratitude:

To Alejandro, Jesus, and Jorge—you know why;

To Pilar Padilla and Hernan Ruiz for the images
and cartoons that animate this work;

To Flavio Rojo Pons, proofreader of all my texts and commentator
of every paper I have published, for your patient and wise voice;

To Patricia Rubio for her translation into English;

And to James Simson for his patience and fine
work in correcting the first draft.

Chapter 1
Inner Team Coaching

Before writing these lines, I followed many paths, always looking for meaningful teachings that would help me better understand myself, my world, and the way I create relationships. Among other things, I was searching for a theory, model, or approach that would so match my needs that I could even "wear it" as a sort of skin that could serve as a kind of new sensory array with which to feel the world.

When I was first confronted with the methodology I will be presenting in this book, I was not yet aware of the way in which my life would change, or how, shortly afterward, this new experience would allow me to go through—like Harry Potter on Platform 9¾—an internal "Berlin Wall" and then be able to cross the real Atlantic Ocean, to return to my country after ten years of living in Germany. I am grateful for the time I spent in that country, since it was there, I must admit, that I faced the worst of my inner prisons; it was also there that I found the path to inner liberation. That path is called inner team coaching, and the process it is based on is called voice dialogue.

All that happened in 1993. While planning my return to Mexico for the following year, I had a second underlying goal of becoming a coach. I wished to be a coach to enable a transformation process in the lives of others that would be as powerful as the one I had experienced. This would be my way of giving back to the world what I had been so privileged to receive.

More than ten years went by until I finally went through training and certification, and I connected with the source of my passion for coaching. This source springs partly from Germany (as an applied methodology) and, as a good child of our time, its mothers and fathers are spread out in different areas of knowledge.

In this section, I am not going to analyze the work of other authors; that is something readers can do for themselves. What I am going to do is introduce, talk with, and listen to the different voices I believe to be significant in understanding the approach and methodology of inner team coaching.

If you are a professional coach looking for new, efficient methodologies, I hope I can awaken your curiosity enough to try out this powerful tool and so enhance your coaching skills. And if you are an executive, a manager, or a corporate officer, I hope to awaken your desire to enter the fascinating world of your own inner life, with the goal of making sure that in all your relationships, your best players appear on the field.

As starting points, I maintain that:

- Not only individuals but also different professional disciplines are shaped and transformed by a wide array of voices. This is especially true for the recently created profession of coaching, nourished by psychology, philosophy, sociology, communication, neuronal and biological research, systems theory, and many more fields of study.

- Coaching, as a profession, nourishes other disciplines and simultaneously takes its substance from voices that, in the furthest case, date back to the centuries before Christ and belong to Buddhist thought.

- The fact that coaching is being built from different approaches, disciplines, and methods does not mean that it lacks a tone and volume of its own. Quite the opposite. Results show that coaching has a voice that has gained in volume, development, and academic interest, resonating and echoing all around the world.

- The value of this new approach to human behavior lies in its capacity to unify and cross-connect contributions to knowledge that, up to now, have been separated from each other and which, when united, create new, powerful, and inspiring realities that none of them alone would have been able to achieve.

- Sometimes the voice of science—which certainly includes the human and behavioral branches—bars any interpretation that would contradict the models developed to explain that which it considers "the truth." Coaching, in return, recognizes the existence of as many truths as there are minds and voices on the planet. It brings understanding to diversity.

- All the voices that exist within a human being are welcome and serve the purposes of coaching. Whatever a person has been, whether an engineer, accountant, architect, hippie, nomad, ecologist, mother, father, rebel, or missionary in the jungle, each position adds to the person's "capital of voices," thanks to which a coach will be able to listen and empathize with the clients in his or her waiting room. In other words, life experience is an important asset that each person brings to coaching.

- We live our lives clinging to what we believe is our identity, as if it were fixed and unchanging. For example, what makes a cat a cat and not something else? Is it fur, paws, genetics, whiskers, or is it the way it leaps, its purring, or the fact that it hunts birds? If I try to take one of these features and blow it up in an attempt to define what it is that separates it from other species, I will be making a serious mistake. It is the interdependence of *all its parts* that makes it a cat. It is not just the sum of its parts that gives it its identity, but more the specific way it relates to other cats and its environment, resulting in the furry animal we call a cat. By the same token, we human beings—incorporating more variables—are brought into being by a vast series of interrelated elements. So if I only wanted to describe myself in terms of one part, I would be guilty of oversimplification and diminishing myself and my view of life. Does an "intelligent" person exist who doesn't, somewhere, have a "dumb part"? Who hasn't had the experience of being dumb in a certain way, situation, or routine? Is it possible to be only useless or a do-nothing or to be good or a hard worker? If the reader is interested in pursuing the matter further, he or she can delve into Buddhist teachings, Greek philosophy, literature, contemporary psychology, or biology. What interests me is reexamining this concept we have grown up with of having a fixed personality, i.e., "I am this way", which we then cling to, thinking it is who we are. The result is that we deny or hide half—or more—of what we really are. In the end, we tend to believe in this reductionist version of our true selves and so limit our capacity to develop our highest potential.

- Is there a better approach to the multiple realities of our planet than one that can reconcile our inner diversity, embrace it, and then take it forward to create new levels of awareness, which would enable us to work from the very depth of what it means to be human?

As I said earlier, these are my starting points. They mean something to me and resonate with my experience of life. I am sharing these points for those who see their sense and meaning in terms of the implications they bring for their coaching practice and their lives.

Chapter 2
The Announcement

One morning, the operations manager, Miguel's direct boss, called him into his office to tell him that after a performance review, the board members had decided to offer him coaching.

Miguel and his boss had already talked about the opportunity for him to be promoted and how hiring a coach was the way the company would go about this. They were both aware of how important it was within the company's culture to make career plans. The board feared Miguel would become a bottleneck for the staff under him and that it would quickly be necessary to find something suitable for him.

The operations manager summed things up in the following way: "I've already told you many times that as a manager, you need to do some medium-term planning, not just spend your time taking care of the everyday workload and carrying on like a firefighter every time there's an emergency.

"You should learn how to delegate and stop doing everything yourself. Assign concrete plans and specific tasks to your staff, and then keep track of them.

"You should be basing your decisions on accurate information that you collect, instead of deciding on the spur of the moment.

"I notice that you avoid focusing on difficult tasks and making complex decisions, that you would rather waste your time on things that your staff could take care of.

"I need to see you working as a team player together with the rest of your colleagues. You need to clearly understand that the Production area, of which you are the leader, can only function if you coordinate with quality, maintenance, logistics, and engineering.

"What about your English? How is it going? You know only too well that at the next level, 80 percent of our business is done directly with Germany and that the board meetings are held in English. Are you keeping up with your lessons?

"So, Miguel, I hope you get some help from the coaching. Failing that, your growth possibilities in the company will be quite limited."

Amen.

Suddenly, Miguel felt as if he had been kicked out of heaven and thrown into purgatory. His boss's view contrasted sharply with his profound conviction that he was already at the "summit of his career." He had never given a thought to the idea that there could be something beyond what he was doing at that moment.

A summit is a summit! Right? he thought. *What difference does it make? I'm already there!*

Barely noticed, another voice popped up—as if from another self. It was like the voice of an imp on his shoulder, and it said, "This definitely has something to do with your problem with Mauricio—that unpleasant quality manager, that cocky junior, puffed up with his private-school background, who is always trying to find a way to make you look bad so he can feel superior. All you do is complain and criticize him because deep down you believe he really is better than you—"

"But there's a big difference between having a conflict with him and being a bottleneck ... which means they could take me off at the neck. This is just not fair. I am the one always looking for ways to solve all these problems plus being burdened with everything going on around me just to achieve the goals!" said another of his inner voices, coming to his defense.

Miguel simply stopped breathing, and sweat started running down his temples. It seemed that his inner voices were in revolt. Each one claimed to be right, leaving him feeling stunned, frozen, and lost. The more they spoke in his ears, the smaller he felt. The louder they were, the more fragile and vulnerable he became.

Oh, I wish the earth would just swallow me up!

Suddenly, he recalled the image of that day back in high school, when the physics teacher had humiliated him before the whole class for giving the wrong answer to a question. He was so embarrassed that all he wanted to do was dig a deep hole and stick his head in it, like an ostrich.

"If I was a successful manag—" said one voice from his inner orchestra that wanted to speak up but was drowned out by another one that roared in his ears. This was a voice he immediately recognized, having heard it over and over throughout his entire life.

"You're not worthy, not good enough. You just don't deserve anything. The child can leave the fields, but the fields never leave the child, isn't that so?

"How do you always react when you have to make a presentation in front of guests from Germany or the United States? You just stand there, paralyzed, stutter more than usual, and then start blushing. That goes on until that hated Mauricio 'the junior' shows up and saves the day, speaking his incredibly fluent English while cutting you to pieces with his over-whelming superiority."

A new thought entered his head.

So, is it all a lie? Am I an impostor? Oh, God, what happens if I can't do what they expect of me? Will I get fired? What about my parents? And my sisters? What about my wife and children? And all those depending on my income? I'd rather die! No, no, no!

It was time for the suspicious voice to come back in.

"A coach. What's that? Where did they get her from? Is she in some way a personal spy for the manager? Or does she come from HR? Maybe she is one of those consultants who recommend layoffs once the staff members have coughed up their 'secrets'? So, as a plan, the best thing for me is to be suspicious. I'll have to watch my tongue with that coach."

When he got home that evening, he was so tense while taking a glass from the cupboard for a drink of water that he smashed the glass and badly cut his finger. He ended up getting stitches in the emergency room.

That night, several hours later, just before the painkiller finally helped him get to sleep, he heard one of his many inner voices whispering, "You will pay in blood ..."

Chapter 3
Voices That Left a Trace

In the same manner that the body takes form within the mother's womb, so is man's consciousness awakened and surrounded by the consciousness of others.

—Mikhail Bakhtin

With the aim of exploring our inner diversity as human beings, I am going to recount some events from my personal life that are easy to remember. I will refer them to quotes from the authors of the "Inner Team Model," from philosophy, from psychology, and from literature. My intention is to show how their material has come to life in my own experience.

One of the oldest memories I have goes back to when I was five years old. My sister—the fourth in a family of five, of which I am the youngest—had recently started elementary school in a big educational center run by nuns, where every day she heard about the distinction between "good" and "evil" and came to feel the urge to "save me," given the fact that I didn't know things that the "older ones" did.

This was the day she explained to me, very seriously, how "pagans go to hell and burn in eternal fire." At this moment, she ordered me to forever stop stealing cookies during the evening while my mother was distracted and far from the kitchen. She said that those were "acts of the devil" and that if I did not quit doing them, I would burn for eternity. She, as the "older one," was bound to protect me from such danger, at least until I could go to school and be indoctrinated. At that same moment, she swore that she would "never, ever, ever" take the pantry keys again, so I decided to continue stealing by myself, in total secrecy. That conversation introduced my fragile conscience not only to the moral aspect of my actions—innocent though they were at that time—but also set a precedent as to which games I could be open about and which ones would be secret in my life; the obedient voice was overlaid by a rebellious voice that refused to believe the story about hell.

What I want to take from this event is the fact that I was able to get in touch—at that time and place and for the first time, consciously, more or less—with the experience of duality, polarity, contrast, and contradiction: on one side, a carefree little girl acting spontaneously and following her impulses, on the other, the sister who I learned later would show up to teach the corresponding lessons. I was letting in a voice that, in due course, became a basic part of my life. Many years later, I formally named my original voice Pinocchio and my sister's Jiminy Cricket. The latter was to become the voice of my consciousness; its job was to process the morality of everything I did. What I want to get across is that for a long time, this voice was hers; however, inadvertently, it got mixed in with mine until it became part of the chorus of voices that make me what I am today.

> Everything related to me comes into my consciousness, beginning with my name, from the external world and through the words of others, with their emotional and evaluative tonality. We appraise ourselves from the perspective of others; we intend to know ourselves through others; we perceive our outward features through the eyes of others, we orient our behavior regarding others; we build our own speech referring the speech of others, entwined with it, in response to it, and anticipating future replies. In the same sense and due to our "outwardness" with respect of others, we possess a portion of the latter, capable of completing a "vision surplus" that is accessible only for us by virtue of our position regarding others. This is how, with the assistance of the others, the ego can build its own identity.[2]

---

[2] García, "Identidad y alteridad en Bajtín,"

Voices can also enter us through songs, and they remain as recordings in the cultural memory bank, which is what happened with the national anthem of Costa Rica, my mother's country, which, through repetition, was engraved in my cultural memory bank. It was as though I were a resident of the heaven on earth she came from, and to where, as her daughter, I could be transported through the "stories by Aunt Panchita" and her traditional songs.

When it was time for me to go to grammar school—yes, to the same institution as my sister, with the nuns—I became aware of other highly seductive voices, like French, for example. I learned there were other languages apart from my own. To discover that I could describe a bird singing in the window in such a beautiful way by saying, *"L'oiseaux chante à la fenêtre"* was both magical and fun.

With the arrival of language came my own unique way of listening to and imitating sounds. However, what had the greatest effect were those snippets of foreign culture, reinforced by listening, reciting, and repetition, which were to become part of me. The *"Marseillaise"* joined up with the *"Massiosare"* (the popular name given to the Mexican national anthem, referring to the sound of one of its verses: *"Más si osare ..."*), along with the Costa Rican national anthem. A cluster of homelands came to live inside me without my permission, to which I felt I should show loyalty when asked. In this way, plurality, diversity, and variety became key elements of my identity.

> No thought can be abstracted from its original context or the network of liaisons that give it form. Therefore, it's not a matter of stating—as Ortega y Gasset claimed—"I am myself and my circumstance"; but more clearly, "I am myself with the other in our circumstance."
>
> —José Alejos García

Other voices that left a deep mark in me came from literature. Regardless of being a bit too young to fully understand it, I read *Demian* by Hermann Hesse, a book that stayed anchored in my heart. I saw myself as in a mirror, in that dual world populated by manipulating Abels who profited from their victim status and stigmatized Cains who, deep inside, were more honest than those who proclaimed themselves "good." Absorbed in Hesse's world, I then devoured *Steppenwolf*, which further increased the range of selves living within me.

Even today, when I read it, I can only reaffirm how much sense his description makes to me.

> In fact, none of my selves—not even the most naive one—is a unit, but a highly multi-shaped world; a small heaven of stars, a chaos of shapes, shades, and states, legacies, and possibilities. Let each one of them individually make the effort to mistake this chaos for a unit and talk about his own self, as if it was a simple phenomenon, solidly made and clearly outlined: this illusion, natural to all men (even the most elevated ones) seems to be a necessity, a demand of life, just like breathing and eating are (…).
>
> Illusion relies on a simple passage. As a body, each man is one; as a soul, never (…) Man is an onion with one hundred layers, a weave made by multiple threads.[3]

"An illusion," says Hesse. In western society, we grow up with the idea of being a type of solid being, an "I," and as a result, we get stuck to the ideas we have of ourselves. This identity-building process starts when we assume our own name and everything it means. The identity created by someone named Moses will differ depending on whether his father, grandfather, and great-grandfather had the same name or if he is the first one in the family to be called Moses.

A series of properties get added to the name, qualities and characteristics that gradually acquire volume and consistency as we grow older. The voices we hear during childhood that continually affirm something about us suddenly turn into reality, not just in what we do, but especially in our minds. Thus, if Moses repeatedly heard: "You're smart, generous, and considerate," his sense of identity would grow solidly along those lines, up to the point where he would accept the affirmation as a universal and unquestionable truth. His choices in life and his way of relating to others

---

[3] Hermann Hesse, *Steppenwolf.*

would be naturally imbued with a sense of what "is possible" within the framework from which he derives his identity. On the other hand, if what Moses heard repeatedly were comments like: "You're useless, careless, and inconsiderate," and he took them for himself, it is likely that his adult behavior will conform to this view, and the type of relationship he'll create with the world will only serve to reinforce it.

In our minds, we start creating what are known as "mental models,"[4] or maps that help us journey through life and explain the things that happen around us. Since our early stages of development, we have been learning to meet our basic needs for affection, attention, care, and approval in ways that result in greater or lesser success. We believe in the illusion that "the way we were born" is "the way we are" and "the way we are" is "the way we will always be." If we add this to some sort of family or cultural conditioning with a specific bias involving "genetic factors," then we prove that events can only turn out one way. We hear this in sentences like: "Birds of a feather … ;" "The Simsons have always had strong personalities;" and "The men in this family never come to a good end."

With this type of map, the possibilities for learning are limited. We reduce ourselves to mere receptacles of what the map would have us be and we reject everything that goes against, questions, or broadens it. The more we believe in this rigid behavior, the less open we are and the more ready we become to take up arms to defend the person we think we are, instead of the one we think we are not.

---

[4] The concept of "mental models" was coined by the Scotsman Kenneth Craik in the forties and defines them as:

"Deeply rooted beliefs, images and assumptions that we have about ourselves, our world, our organizations, and how we fit in with them". Here are the principles of 'mental models':

1. We all have them.
2. They determine how and what we see, how we think and act.
3. They lead us to believe that our inferences are facts.
4. They are always incomplete.
5. They influence the effects of our actions, and are thus self-fulfilling.
6. They frequently outlive their usefulness.
7. We are violently resistant to changing or questioning them.

So far, we have the following keys to the puzzle:

1. What we refer to as "our identity" is not the same as our "being." Identity is the "history" or version that we have built of who we are, and it has been limited since the outset.
2. Having over-identified with characteristics we think of as "self" leads us to a limited map of reality that, in turn, will influence our opportunities for growth and transformation.
3. Those features with which we identify ourselves undoubtedly find contrast in their opposites, those features that we disown. Intelligence stands out thanks to its opposite, stupidity; light and dark, good and evil, head and tail, heaven and earth. "Countless pairs of poles," as Hermann Hesse said.
4. It is possible to move away from what we believe we are, in order to separate the "self" from "the story" that we have created. It is in separating and moving away that we discover that the "I am" is not that single quality or feature, but a lot more. That's where we become open to transformational learning.
5. At present, there are well-known biologists like Bruce Lipton, who, in his book *Biology of Belief*, confirms all of the above, basing his findings on cellular and molecular research. He defies the genetic determinism that we believe ourselves to be victims of and suggests ways for us to modify our thoughts in order to change our destiny. Others, such as Humberto Maturana, base their approaches on cultural biology.

Here, the reader might ask himself: "How many opposing versions of myself am I able to find?"

Chapter 4
Who Is Miguel?

Miguel Antonio Hernández Pérez is thirty-five years old. He was born in La Damiana, Michoacán, a community so small that it seems only its inhabitants know about it. He is portly and thick-set like a barrel, has a short neck, and it looks like all of his muscles are in a state of permanent tension. He has a round face and wide cheeks, big eyes, and a frozen smile. He avoids eye contact and walks with clenched fists and a slight crouch, as if he is carrying a great weight on his shoulders. His hair grows like the tines on a fork and is always covered with hair gel. His wife tells him that he grows grass instead of hair. He used to have an Argentinean colleague who called him "Manolito" and even got him a volume of *Mafalda* so he would understand why. The firstborn of his parents' twelve children, Miguel arrived in this world to continue the family line and, like his father and grandfather before him, become a mariachi player. This was what he was going to be; in the meantime, he helped out in the fields with the rest of the children. He lived in a poor area, where there wasn't enough to eat, especially in times of drought, when even the corn needed for tortillas could not be had. From his perspective as a child, he could not understand why he was the last one to be fed. In his own mind, the fact that his stomach was bigger than those of his siblings meant he should have proportionately more to eat. Instead, having been left the last scraps from the table, he ended up with an aching emptiness that was worse than outright hunger.

In this often bleak scene, the Hernandez family stood out from others because of one special feature: namely, the intense effort made by the parents to educate each child to his or her own place in the family's orchestra, where they each played a different instrument. That wasn't all they learned: their mother taught them to dance and to sing during the long, peaceful, sunny days in the fields, which seemed endless to them.

Thanks to their skill, the Hernandezes were given the role of providing the entertainment during community *fiestas* and religious ceremonies. They gradually became known to neighboring towns and received more invitations to play. Slowly but surely, the parents achieved their dream of a better standard of living.

Miguel sang solo. Young girls cheered at the sound of his voice, and his mother dreamed that one day, her son might even sing with the Mariachi Vargas de Tecalitlán, the most famous mariachi orchestra in the world. Miguel did not share his mother's dream. He wanted to continue with his education and finish high school. His father did everything in his power to convince him that the only way he could contribute to the family was by singing. He mistreated Miguel and interfered with his learning by finding any number of extra chores for him, thus preventing him from doing his homework. Miguel had to wake up before dawn to do his homework secretly, at the back of the house near the latrine.

He got into high school, not knowing what this would cost him personally. During those three years, he lived with another type of emptiness in his gut, not caused by a lack of bread, but from longing to be accepted and included.

When he approached groups of peers during recess, some would mock him, while others would steal his pencils from his schoolbag to show him who was boss. He was assaulted, beaten up, and discriminated against. From that point on, he learned well that it was better to keep his eyes down, to submit, to avoid being noticed; his motto was: "Keep quiet, so nobody notices you," and the most important thing he learned was to hide his anger in situations where he couldn't win.

Meanwhile, his parents missed the most talented member of the orchestra.

Having finished high school, Miguel woke up one morning certain of one thing, which was that he wanted to be an engineer. He faced his father after his graduation ceremony and gave him his decision. He would go to college and attend technical school. There was no power on earth that could get him to change his mind. In a last-ditch effort, Miguel's father bought him a new guitar and asked him to come and join the orchestra during the school holidays. He wanted Miguel to come and play at the weddings and sweet-sixteen parties that had been booked. He hoped Miguel would be reminded of his origins and where he'd got his music from—the music that was supposed to be his passion—and would be persuaded that his future lay right there in Damiana and not in the big cities where he'd just be a nobody.

His efforts were in vain. Miguel was no longer a child. He had developed the skills of a survivor and knew what he had to do to move forward. He won a scholarship for college. He was unaware of where it would take him, and each step pulled him farther away from what his father had hoped for him and brought him closer to his own dream of becoming an engineer.

Lives move, shift, and evolve; a lot happened in Miguel's life, and in 2001, after submitting his résumé to dozens of companies in central Mexico, he was selected for an interview and finally hired by a German automotive company with a manufacturing plant in Silao, Guanajuato. He had just graduated and was not expecting much in the way of salary or position; he began demonstrating his ability "at the coalface."

What is interesting to note is how the number three plays a part in the timing of his life. It was as though the three years of high school, followed by three years of college, had set a precedent. He completed his technical degree in twelve terms and started work as a maintenance engineer, which lasted three years with rotating shifts every three months. He was promoted to production-line supervisor, which he did for three years until he was offered the post of manufacturing manager.

The night of his first day as manager, Miguel and his wife conceived the first of their three children, who were born exactly one year after the other.

In the company, Miguel is known as "The Fireman" because he is always in a sweat, carrying on his shoulders the burden of all the problems in production and the responsibility to fix each of them at once. He is the last to leave, sometimes after 10:00 p.m., and he is often seen charging around on the weekend—twice as fast, because he is keen to get back home to his wife and children. His wife is always complaining that his devotion to work has made him a ghost at home.

"It's not as if anyone is going to thank you for it," she once told him angrily.

Nevertheless, he feels that's the way it has to be with his responsibility as a manager and that every day, he needs to prove his commitment by meeting production deadlines.

The only time he has to himself is while driving to and from work, when he takes the road between Leon and Silao and the brand-new Delta Boulevard around the city. He likes the view as he drives past the few fields that remain for farming and the rural communities. Sometimes, after spending the night in a sweat going over and over unsolvable plant issues in his mind, he manages to turn off the radio, take a deep breath, and sense a sort of release on his way to work.

However, despite all his efforts, he feels weighed down by his workload and his family obligations.

His wife is constantly pushing him to find another job with a better salary. What she doesn't realize is that nearly half of his income goes to meet other costs.

"It's none of her business what I earn or how I spend it," he tells himself. Five of his seven brothers immigrated illegally to the United States long ago and he hasn't heard from them since. He is helping his two youngest sisters with their careers and religiously sends money to his parents.

His parents had to flee Damiana in 2009. The Michoacana Family cartel, known as the "Malillos" (bad guys), took over, and fighting over the territory began with the "Zetas" gang and the "Others"—the army. They now live in Apatzingan, where, although the profession is in decline, his father has managed to get taken on by a local mariachi band. What has made things worse is that there has been an increase in shootings at weddings, putting Miguel's father at grave risk. At one wedding, a burst of gunfire hit the musician next to him. The music of La Negra was underscored by screams, shots, and the lifeless body of poor Samuel, the trumpet player.

Miguel begs his father to stop taking risks and to live on the money he sends, but his father stubbornly believes that dying while playing music would be the best way to leave this life.

In the company, no one knows about Miguel's private life or his background. It's not a matter for conversation, and he would never volunteer such information for fear that someone would use it to show that he wasn't the right person for the job.

Who knows what the German bosses would do if they learned about this? thinks Miguel, keeping his mouth firmly shut.

Chapter 5
Learning as the Path

> People can do anything, no matter how preposterous it
> may be, to avoid facing their own souls.
>
> —Carl Jung

The process of learning has been studied by almost every available discipline and approach. As a lot has been said already, why do we need to say more when talking about coaching? Not only because the coach lives a life of continuous learning, but also because the nature of the coaching relationship itself is an act of learning.

Coaching is a discipline with increasing presence and relevance worldwide. It represents a key area that traditional adult training does not cover. It is key, because it understands learning from the subject's perspective as something more than just the passive reception of knowledge passed down by experts and teachers.

The learning area covered by coaching can be tied to what the Russian psychologist Lev Vygotsky, one of the founders of social-development theory, called the "zone of proximal development." For individuals and groups, this area or zone is defined as:

> The distance between the actual developmental level as
> determined by independent problem solving and the level
> of potential development as determined through problem
> solving under guidance, or in collaboration with more
> capable peers. Between the "zone of actual development"

and "the zone of potential development" there is "the zone of near development" which is:

The space in which, because of the interaction with others and their assistance, a person can work and resolve an issue or perform a given task in a way and with a level that would have been unachievable if working individually.[5]

If we break this concept down, we discover the following elements that tie in with coaching:

- The starting point for learning is the "zone of actual development" and refers to our current situation. We could also call this our "comfort zone," for it is where we remain comfortable. We don't need to concentrate too much or spend a lot of energy to succeed here. We have the mental routines to demonstrate what we have learned, and we can easily repeat our behavior without outside support.
- Besides that, we all have a "zone of potential development" that we are able to develop as individuals and as part of the groups we belong to. To enter this area of growth, we will need to activate the motors of need, curiosity, will, desire to achieve, risk-taking, and determination. This area of potential development gives us the opportunity for our minds to grow, evolve, transform, and expand and with that, we become more effective.
- Thanks to the involvement of others (in this case, the coach), we can reach a level of clarity and awareness that would not otherwise have been possible. The voice of another works like a mirror; it represents accompaniment, understanding, validation, appreciation, and encouragement as we move from the actual to the potential, or in other words from who we are to who we can be.

Outside the zone of potential development lies the panic zone, where it stops being pleasant and becomes painful and stressful. It's where we get

---

[5] Vygotsky, Lev: *Thought and Language*

in touch with our incompetence and can be overwhelmed by fear, anxiety, and insecurity. It's that place where we put in too much effort for a poor result, where we see others get better results in a third of the time it takes us. We start to feel that we are putting in far more than we are getting back. It's where we can get sick; it's a danger zone with a warning label.

A few years ago, I coached a corporate manager. He was an engineer, a man of action and a very effective manager who had worked for more than fifteen years in different manufacturing areas of the company. He had already been at a new design and planning post for about a year when we started the coaching. He was going downhill. He was staying at work until 10:00 p.m., and his work was never really done. His relationships with team members and coworkers were getting worse every day.

This happened because he had been "shoved" into his panic zone. He didn't feel competent working with the computer software needed for the job. He knew that his planning skills were limited, and so, out of the fear of making a mistake, he wore himself down trying to control even the smallest thing. He was afraid to ask questions about things that seemed obvious to others, and he isolated himself to avoid being seen as weak. He couldn't sleep at night and suffered an alarming level of stress. Coaching helped him to recognize all the elements leading to his exhausted state and to reconsider his position within the company. As part of this process, he met with the director and shortly afterward was reassigned to operations, where he was successful in developing his potential without endangering his physical or mental stability.

In this example, it may seem obvious; however, in daily life, the only thing we can take for granted is that nothing is obvious.

In a coaching relationship, it is especially important to keep the principle in mind that nothing is obvious. The coach needs to develop the sensitivity to correctly identify the grounds for intervention that will lead the client to his zone of potential development and identify its border with the panic zone. Coaching, as defined by the International Coaching Federation (ICF) is a respectful relationship, aligned with the client's own agenda and not an agenda decided by the coach.

There are a number of different ways of referring to the type of learning that happens when someone manages to expand his zone of potential growth. Some examples may include "significant learning," "high-performance learning," or "effective learning." But there is an even higher level of learning, which includes higher levels of consciousness; it is known as "transformational learning." Werner Erhard describes it like this:

> Transformation does not merely change our actions, does not merely give us new options from which to choose. Rather, it uncovers the structures of being and interpretation on which we are grounded, often unaware of our grounding on them.
>
> This is the work of transformation: this revealing of ourselves to ourselves, which occurs in a profound way that alters the very possibility of being that we are.
>
> In transformation, we bring forth the possibility of creating ourselves, so that life is a creative expression of our stand.[6]

What occurs in the inner team coaching is a transformational learning process. It reveals our being to ourselves. The limited version of what we believe ourselves to be gets significantly expanded. We become aware of the many selves within, which have been hidden or silenced. We discover the power of transformation while becoming owners, accountable for our inner life. We obtain access to the opposing inner voices and the energies they represent. It is not only a matter of recognizing their existence or sensing the way they take charge automatically, but rather of embracing their diversity and developing a process of awareness that enables us to act on them and make conscious choices as to how they will be integrated into our life. This type of learning transforms us while revolutionizing our sense of identity. It changes us from being victims of our unconscious impulses into aware individuals capable of consciously choosing who we are and how we want to relate to ourselves and others.

Here are some questions for the reader to ask him- or herself:

1. So, who do I think I am?
2. Who do I think I am not?

---

[6] Erhard, Werner, Audiobook

3. What is the mindset I use to distinguish between what I say I am vs. what I say I am not?
4. Where did I learn that I am this ... and not the other?

Mirror, dear mirror, what do you have to show me?

Our mind works like a mirror; it projects onto the external reality what we really carry inside. Thus, I only notice a feature in someone else because that same feature resides within me and I see it magnified—or distorted—in that other person. In psychology, this effect is known as "projection." This is a key element in understanding the dynamics of our inner selves.

The Wisdom of the Mirror

First law of the mirror
All the things I would like to change in someone else, all those things that annoy, anger, irritate, or infuriate me about that person ... are things I have in myself.

Second law of the mirror
Everything about me that someone else criticizes, fights against, or tries to change that causes me pain is mine. They are things that I haven't yet resolved, issues for me to work on.

Third law of the mirror
Everything that someone else complains about, criticizes, or tries to change in me that doesn't touch or affect me is a reflection of that person: it's their personality or shortcoming projected onto me.

Fourth law of the mirror
Everything I like about someone and all that I love in someone is also in me. I have it in me and I value it in others. I reflect myself in others, and at this point, I watch myself projected in them.

We seldom like what we see when we look at ourselves in the mirror. We automatically start criticizing what we see. In this sense, our response is understandable when "the other" shows up in the role of "the projection" and blatantly gives us a demonstration of the behaviors we fight against and object to. If we launch a crusade against, for example, irresponsibility, we might find it hard to accept those elements within ourselves that could be characterized as irresponsible. We violently refuse to take ownership of something that we are fighting against. How often do we hear our own judgment proclaim, "Never in my life could I have done such a thing"? It is with the same strength of conviction that we refuse to accept that "such a thing" is also part of our nature. We place ourselves at one pole to judge the opposing part.

In a contrasting example, if we idolize someone, what our mind is really doing is projecting a fantasy that exists only in the mind. As we get to know that person better, the idealized version comes crashing down and we can slip into hatred, disappointment, and rejection. We demonize the other. However, this person is neither divinity nor demon, just him- or herself. The rest of it was our projection.

Here are some things the reader could ask him/herself:

1. What angers me most about others?
2. Who is angry inside me?
3. What criticisms get through to me?
4. Who, inside of me, feels hurt by such criticism?

The Legend of the Empty Cup

According to an old legend, a famous warrior visited the house of a Zen teacher. Upon arriving, he introduces himself and mentions all his credentials and the learning he has gained during long years of sacrifice and study. After such an impressive introduction, he explains that he has come to see him because he wants to learn the secrets of Zen knowledge. As an answer, the teacher simply invites him to take a seat and offers him a cup of tea. Appearing to be absentminded and without showing the smallest concern, the teacher pours tea in the warrior's cup and continues doing so even after the cup is full. Puzzled, the warrior tells the teacher that the cup is full and that the tea is spilling over the table. The teacher answers peacefully, "Precisely, sir. Your cup is already full. How could you possibly learn anything?" Aware of the disbelief in the warrior's face, the teacher emphasizes, "There's nothing you can learn, unless your cup is empty."

Ask yourself:

1. What is my cup full of?
2. What would I have to change in order to be open to a transforming experience or to have an empty cup?
3. What is holding me back?

Being is impossible without the other. Hence, the need to reconsider identity as a social phenomenon, a result of being with yourself and being with others. The other precedes the self, feeding, instructing and accompanying it for a lifetime. We derive our value from how others value us. We seek to know ourselves through the other and see our outsides through the eyes of the other. We modify our behavior in relation to others; we organize our speech from the speech of others, woven in with it, our own speech referring to the speech of others, entangled with it, replying to it and in anticipation of its future replies.[7]

---

[7] García Alejos, *Identidad y alteridad en Bajtin*

Chapter 6
The Preliminary Crisis

Miguel was more taciturn than usual for several days; his inner voices had grown louder and were interrupting and overlapping each other. His attention to daily tasks grew less every day. Away from home, he would drive his car in "automatic" mode and stay awake all night. To add to the wound he had already gotten on his right hand, he had also banged his head against a rack in the company's warehouse. The bruise, which was impossible to conceal, made him look like he'd been punched in the left eye. "A stone in my path taught me that my fate was to roll and roll," he sang to himself.

Five days later, he received the self-evaluation form that he was to complete as a part of the 360 evaluation for coaching. His first impulse was to give himself a high score in almost every competence. He could not help thinking that quality would take revenge and that Javier from maintenance, who was fond of him, would write positive things, but there was also Ubaldo—a crafty guy from whom you never knew what to expect—and then there was Irving, who was after his job and had started all this mess, and Daniel, the little friend of the abusive manager who certainly wasn't his best bet.

"And … what will the boss have to say about me? He is always yelling and humiliating me in front of everyone. Why it is that he only yells at me and is polite with everyone else? Is it because I have brown skin? Or is it because I studied in public schools? Why doesn't he like me? Why? Why hasn't he said something? Respect is supposed to be an important rule in this company, and he does not respect me," Miguel asked himself over and over.

He erased what he had written and then gave himself an even higher score on several behaviors. Why not? After all, he was the one carrying the whole thing. Nobody else gave as much time or effort. He often worked on the weekends. He was the only one to work late solving the problems left by his team.

I must defend myself, whatever happens, he thought, and immediately, one of his voices piped up.

"Don't you see what a disaster you are? How can you give a score of five in 'teamwork', when it's really just chaos and no one works as a team? Put a two, tops." So Miguel lowered his scores for every single item.

It took him two hours to complete the questionnaire. He changed his scores over and over again, without managing to make a single one of his voices happy; they just continued arguing. Not satisfied with the final outcome, he saved the file. He didn't send it, just as he hadn't sent many other files about meetings and halfway done projects that lay dormant in his hard drive as testament to his indecision.

The next day, with some prompting from Human Resources, who needed the information for processing, he managed to send the questionnaire, with a few changes.

Throughout the day, Miguel spent some time studying each one of his colleagues, trying to read their minds and find out how they had evaluated him. He hated them all. *Why do they have to be on the planet?* he wondered.

The night before his first session, he could not sleep.

"What's the matter, Miguel?" his wife asked.

"Nothing. Go back to sleep," he replied.

Nothing ... nothing ... What if there was something?

The woman's complaint was only heard by her pillow.

The following day, for the first time ever, Miguel felt the physical consequences of his turbulent inner dialogue. He woke up with an earache from the racket of all those hours of arguing he'd put up with and no way of lowering the volume in order to sleep.

Chapter 7
The Model

> When you are by yourself, observe your mind.
> When you are around people, observe your speech.
>> —Buddhist tradition from Tibet Kadampa

What actually are these "souls within our breast"? We know they are dynamic units of energy that contain a request, make themselves heard on particular occasions, and take up inner space. As a message or impulse, they can go straight "into action."

Psychological literature uses a range of names for these participants in our inner activity:

- subpersonalities, or, in abbreviated form, parts (Schwartz 1997)
- voices (Bach and Torbet 1985; H. and S. Stone 1989)
- selves (H. and S. Stone 1989)
- elements (of personality) (Assagioli 1993)
- inner persons (Orban 1996)
- inner team members (Schulz von Thun, 1998)

Out of them all, there is no doubt that Hal and Sidra Stone are known as the mother and father of inner-voice exploration (voice dialogue). Coming from a Jungian base and creating their own discipline, The Psychology of Selves, they have developed the most intensive lifelong journey of discovery possible on any side of our inner world. There are professionals from diverse backgrounds who have based their models on the Stones' work.

One of them is the inner team model developed in Germany by Schulz von Thun. The goal of working with inner voices is to achieve higher levels of performance by developing a process of awareness while embracing the polarized selves as they fight for a lead role in our inner life.

This model is based on recognition of the fact that as humans, we are born defenseless and vulnerable. We are born with a set of basic needs that have to be met, especially during the first few years of life, and that remain with us for the rest of our lives. Among them, the need for these three things stands out: attention, approval, and affection. *Attention* can be translated to mean someone to look after, care about, and protect us; *approval* can mean to feel that we are worth something and are appreciated; and *affection* is demonstrated in every possible form: physical, emotional, verbal, and nonverbal.

A baby quickly learns to react whenever a need is not being met. For instance, he learns that a lot of crying brings a frown of disapproval to mother's face, and he learns that it is better to smile if he wants to be cherished. In this way, the baby learns from the cradle to please in order to protect himself from the vulnerability that he experiences when he senses rejection or disapproval or has affection withdrawn. This is how we learn compliance, which is just one of the protective mechanisms that will help us meet our needs throughout life. In different developmental stages, other defenses appear, depending on context, culture, and prevalent values. Some of us learn to be hard workers; some of us develop mental skills; and some will develop athletic prowess—all with the aim of meeting the same needs.

What is then hidden by our *personality* underneath these lifelong behaviors?

The most primitive emotion is hidden under the surface: fear. Many authors have devoted their time to analyzing and studying its impact on the mind, body, and emotions of human beings since the very first stages of their development.

Fear is present like no other emotion in the animal kingdom. The sight of a gazelle fleeing from the leopard, the feel of a rabbit trembling when held, or the terrified look in the eyes of a cat as it dashes to safety—they all generate intense movement (*emotion*, from the Latin *motere*).

The way we react to fear inevitably puts us in an antagonistic posture:

here I am, alone and vulnerable; over there, opposing me, is the threat. My automatic response to threat is to behave one way, while my adversary does the opposite. If I run, it attacks; if attacked, it fights or flees.

To make sense of how we are influenced by these "countless pairs of poles," we have two Germans to thank: Fritz Riemann for creating the framework, and Christof Thomann for his work on conflict management. The Cartesian model we grew up with pushes us into the trap of believing that we have to live in a uni-polar world; where opposites are excluded, banished, or unimaginable—not a part of. It's unthinkable or incompatible. I am good or I am bad; I am pretty or I am ugly. Following this logic, we take a position from which we declare war on all that represents the "opposite," for its mere existence threatens our security. Therefore, those that are like us, those that belong to "our group" are the good guys. No matter where we actually put ourselves. it will always be like that. This is because our mind divides, separates, and excludes, using the linear rationale that has been drummed into us.

Some time ago, I read something about the process of breathing, which has two parts: inhaling and exhaling. Suppose we decide that inhaling is "good," because when we take air into our bodies, we give ourselves life; we absorb energy. Inhaling means living, and we want to live. We want to live a lot. We want to take in more life, so we take in more air. On the other hand, exhaling is death. We get rid of toxins from the body when we exhale, and we give up a bit of life each time we breathe out. Seen this way, exhaling is "bad," so we opt only for the "good" and reject the "bad." We inhale deeply, more and more each breath, to fill ourselves with life. We'll only inhale and not do the "bad" thing because that will take us closer to death. The problem is that if we keep inhaling without exhaling, we are sure to see our lungs burst and then we really will die.

However, if we consider inhaling and exhaling as two elements that complement each other, that are part of a process in which neither is good nor bad, we don't have to choose one and reject the other one. We just breathe. No judgments. Let's transfer this example to other concepts like fast and slow, work and leisure, action and passivity, affirmation and denial. When we look at all these as part of a cycle that needs both to be whole, what happens then in our minds? One cannot exist without the other.

Riemann identifies four basic fears around which we humans shape our way of being in the world and take on the different voices and selves to accommodate them. These four fears are to be found at the ends of a matrix that represent *space* and *time*. How we deal with these fears defines our way of relating to the world, what we accept and what we hate, what we are able to do and what is almost impossible.

1. Space, or the paradox between dependence and autonomy

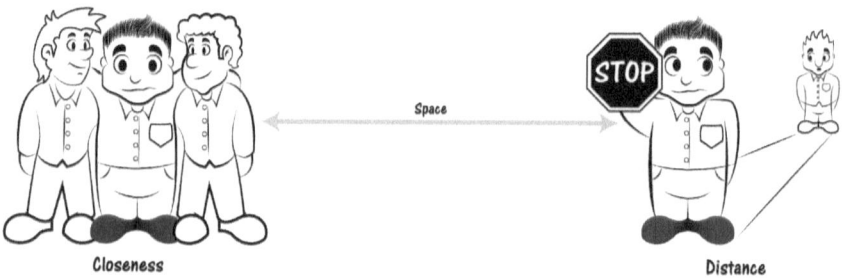

Closeness   Distance

A human being inhabits space that is fixed, and his relationships are influenced by the way in which he deals with space. Looking at it this way, we see that there are individuals who have a greater need for closeness to others (for personal or cultural reasons) or a greater need for distance in their dealings with others.

This is where the first pair of poles can be identified.

Closeness

The need for closeness is linked to the desire for attention, company, sharing, belonging, and harmony—to fit in and to feel valued by others. The person at this pole of the axis is someone willing to cooperate, who gives selflessly to others, who is empathetic and ready to participate. He seeks balance, love, and loyalty. He is ready to obey others and expects to be directed. He cares for others and wants to be cared for. Being depended on by others gives him a feeling of security. One of his greatest needs is to belong.

A person's primary voice or self is developed at this pole, when his main fear is to lose the security of belonging to a group. He is afraid of becoming autonomous. In his world, the other, the "you," has a disproportionate value, leading to dependent relationships.

From this pole, there are two fundamental elements: to love and to need. It is here that we encounter personalities that are either dependent on others or need others to be dependent on them.

The fear of losing the sense of belonging is like being thrown into an abyss of abandonment and separation, of being all alone. In the drive for acceptance, this person will go to great lengths and even abandon himself to make sure he belongs.

His response to this can be to idealize others. He is ready to turn a blind eye to their faults in order to avoid tension. He all too easily plays the ostrich, hiding his head in the sand so as not to have to do anything or face unpleasant situations that might pose a risk to his being accepted by, or belonging to, a group. One example of this would be a manager whose main focus is getting on well with others and who consequently neglects results because he can't set limits.

Here, we see his tremendous effort to make sure that he fits in with the groups he belongs to and how his willingness to help and support others can result in him giving up on his own wants and needs.

One valuable lesson someone at this pole needs to learn is about giving and receiving. This means this person needs to understand what he deserves and stop seeing others as being superior to him.

Roles

Devoted
Committed
Good person
Nurturer
Caretaker
Super-parent
Smothering
Victim

Distance

> Your poor self-esteem has made a prison of your loneliness.
>
> —Friedrich Nietzsche

The person who is at the end of this polarity regards his liberty, independence, and autonomy as bastions of his life. He sets limits with others, protects his territory, and lives in his own world, to which only a few have access. He can curb emotional expression even when having intense feelings and can be very sensitive, even if he doesn't show it. This person is consistent, rational, focused on facts, withdrawn, logical, and insecure, while seeming self-assured. He can seem arrogant. If people get closer than is comfortable, he feels threatened. His fear is of losing himself and giving himself over to others.

He would rather go unnoticed and remain anonymous, operating behind the curtain and never in leadership roles. He likes to participate in the lives of others without drawing attention to himself.

Because emotions and feelings bring us closer to others, he tends to dissociate from them and turn them into rational arguments that seem to be objective. He regards love, attraction, and empathy as dangers to his individuality. Frequently, he defends himself by attacking with irony or sarcasm.

Those who live at the end of this axis see the world as dangerous and they protect themselves by keeping their distance. They reject others to avoid being rejected themselves.

The core fear at this pole is lack of trust and extreme vulnerability. Even the right to exist is being questioned.

Roles
Loner
Spartan
Critical mind
Protector
Guarded
Indifferent
Sarcastic
Perfectionist

2. The axis of time, or the paradox between change and stability

The vertical axis represents how we react to time in a broader sense, oscillating between stability and change. Both poles show two opposing tendencies: either the great need for stability and security or its opposite, the need for change as the most exciting thing in life.

Permanence, stability

This is seen as the need for control supported by the doctrine of, "That's the way it is because that's the way it's always been and that's the way it will always be." At this pole, people believe that anything new involves a risk to their personal security and fosters the fear of the unknown. They cling to what they have to make it last, to preserve and maintain it. This saves them from the anguish caused by uncertainty in the face of change.

Those identified at this pole strive for perfection, control, and an optimal state of affairs. They tend also to be obsessive. For them, there is only true or false, what is right and in good order. They are thorough, cautious, focused on performance, tenacious, disciplined, and have the endurance, drive, and willingness to fight for their ideas. They are thrifty, grounded, solid, and reliable. They tend to stick to their habits, because otherwise there would be uncertainty, and uncertainty is the mother of all their fears.

It is true that we all have within us a strong yearning for permanence and consistency. Our habits and our experience

Change

Time

Permanence/Stability

of the familiar keep the world from falling into chaos. If there were no order in the outside world, our inner lives would only know chaos too. All human beings seek permanence and stability to a greater or lesser extent, depending on which polarity we have within us.

So what happens when someone feels an overly intense fear of change? He will try to keep everything the way it has always been. He will search tirelessly for what is absolute and unchanging. He will resist anything that smacks of change and do anything in his power to maintain order.

There are those at the extreme end of this polarity who cling to their daily routine and refuse to let go. Their lives are determined by prejudices that inhibit their development. The principal problem they run into is their exaggerated need for safety. They ponder everything in minute detail, which means they are very slow to reach decisions. They often find themselves in the paradoxical situation of the man who wants to learn to swim before going into the water for the first time. Or the one who has been stopping himself from buying a new computer for ten years, because there might be a new model out next month.

Roles

Defender of law and order

Man of principles

Truth seeker

Know-it-all

Disciplined

Correct

Controller

Change

> Man is a king when he dreams and a beggar when he thinks.
> —Friedrich Hölderlin

Vitality, spontaneity, and creativity characterize this polarity. When a person is living life from this perspective, for which change is inherent to all realities, what generates fear is its opposite; namely, permanence. This fear is experienced as a loss of freedom, the most precious asset. For those who are happy making endless changes, any attempt to stick to tradition, even if it entails a measure of security, can hinder change and so pose a threat to their identity. On one hand, there is openness to change, to explore what is new and to try other ways of doing things. On the other, it can appear as superficial and lacking in maturity, depth, or commitment. At the furthest extreme of this polarity is change for the sake of change, like fashion.

Someone on the end of this polarity fears the repetition and tedium of routine, so he or she experiences an exaggerated need for freedom and change.

This person fears the limitations deriving from the imposition of any kind of rule or regulation. For this person, promises and commitments are not forever. He lives on the basis of, "What's done is done; the past is behind me and I am moving on." He won't plan for the future so as to keep his options open. "What if something interesting comes up?" he tells himself. Life on this pole is an adventure, living in the moment and constantly on the lookout for new stimuli and points of view. He can make himself available at the drop of a hat, and it's not difficult to talk him into doing something if he is in the mood and feels like it.

Those at the end of this pole believe rules are made to be broken.

Behind this fear of freedom we notice the fear of order, ageing, death, social convention, and gender expectations. In other words, anything that speaks of limitation in life.

Punctuality is not their thing, nor is responsibility or rigid moral principles. Everything happens in the moment and is a matter of perspective.

Those who find themselves at the extreme of this pole are "in love with being in love." They have intense, passionate, and demanding relationships. Boredom is unknown to them. Thanks to their nature, they can be the life and soul of the party. They change partners frequently. They are highly competitive and have a strong need to be a one-man band. They feel personal slights and criticism very acutely.

Fernando Pessoa expresses the poetry of this polarity.

I multiplied myself to feel myself,
To feel myself I had to feel everything,

I overflowed, I did nothing but spill out,
I undressed, I yielded,
And in each corner of my soul there's an altar to a different god.[8]

Fear: to appear needy will trigger feelings of hopelessness and threaten personal freedom

<hr />

[8] Bojorquez, Mario: *"Fernando Pessoa: el hombre multitudinario"*

Activity

The aim of this activity is to identify the different polarities and the diversity within yourself in light of some larger themes.

Pick the one that is closest to how you act, think, and make decisions among the following subjects. For each one, find out if you lean toward that pole or its opposite, or if different topics bring forth different sub-personalities from your inner life.

1. Money

Closeness

Money is not really important in life, but I need it to make others happy. When I have cash, I buy small gifts; that way, I always have something to give my friends.

Distance

It is important not to rely on others or ask for things in order to avoid obligation or commitment to others. Money represents independence. When I have to give a present, money is the best thing because the receiver knows better than I do what he wants.

Permanence

Save what you can during the harvest, because you don't know when there'll be a downturn. Keep your savings securely invested for "rainy days" or the unexpected. The best way of ensuring a good life is by carefully managing your money.

Change

People tell me I'm incapable of managing money, and it's not true. In fact, I'm a good spender. I spend more than I make. The truth is that I don't really know if I am in debt or not. When I have money, I'm quite generous: the money's scarcely arrived before it's gone again. Money's no good sitting in a bank.

2. Sexuality

Closeness

Sex is only pleasant if it is part of a lasting and stable relationship in which one feels pampered, loved, and very close to the other. Total surrender and merging with the other gives meaning to sex.

Distance

Sex is great, provided feelings don't get in the way and you can have fun without complicating it with the questions, explanations, or demands of the other. I am excited by the fact that I don't know the other person. The worst thing anyone can do is ask, "Do you love me?"

Permanence

Sexuality can be pleasant, provided the atmosphere is right and happens the way I want. It's not a matter of saying, "Friday evening, always at the same time," but it matters to me that there's some regularity so I can get ready. It's an enjoyable habit.

Change

You've got to have some spice in life. Otherwise, it becomes tasteless and bland. The best sex is spontaneous, experimental, and open to discovery. It's the end when it turns into a routine.

3. Death

Closeness

I'd rather die at home, in my own bed, surrounded by my loved ones, with someone to hold my hand when I say good-bye to it all. The worst would be to die alone in a hospital, plugged into machines, to die with no one around me.

Distance

Death is a personal affair, and I would like to do what Eskimos do, just wander away from their communities to die alone and in peace. However, it would also be good to have professional help within reach in order to deal with severe pain.

Permanence

The most important thing is having the time to get used to the idea: getting ready for death, making funeral service and burial arrangements, signing the will, and making sure everything in order. The last thing I would want is to cause discomfort. It is important that my family members have a list of what to do, with everything in order and in the right place, to make things easier for them.

Change

What? Did you have to pick today to talk to me about this? Wouldn't it be better to spend the time figuring out how to get more and live more intensely in a life that is already too short? To me, the best way to die would be quickly—ideally with a glass of wine in my hand and in an enticing situation.

Chapter 8
The Takeoff

As usual, Miguel was late for his appointment in the company meeting room, the only one with a lock, overlooking the garden. He was going to have his first coaching session. Managers from the plant and Human Resources were there, as well as the coach and the operations manager, his hated boss.

Lennard von Stockelsdorf, the German plant manager, opened the session in his guttural Spanish.

"We are here, Miguel, as you know, because we are continuing to grow as a company and we need you to improve your management skills. For you, this will mean paying attention to how you act and being aware of how you lead the teams. We are going to see significant growth next year, and you need to get a better understanding of your role. Miguel, you need to be ready for this important challenge. That's why we want you to have some coaching."

Von Stockelsdorf took a deep breath, looked at the coach, patted her on the shoulder, and said, "And this is where you come in, Coach." He looked at Miguel again. "So, you see, coaching is not a bad thing. It's quite the opposite. Our aim is for our people to reach the next level of development and performance, to fulfill their potential. This company does not invest in people who do not move forward. I'd like to hear what you have to say, Miguel. How do you feel?"

"No, uh … well, yes … it's totally clear," Miguel replied.

"Look, it's like this," von Stockelsdorf continued. "We don't need you to become a leader, but a leaders' leader, and we want to know if you're going to be able to do that. It's my opinion that managers in this country are almost masochistic, and you're a perfect example of this. You are a hard worker and make a real effort, which is good. But a manager is supposed to be managing. You don't get paid for doing the work yourself and for fixing machines. I do not pay you to do other people's jobs and then spend your weekends here. I pay you to plan the work for others." He paused, milking the drama out of the moment. "I pay you to be a manager. You do not have to force yourself into it; just adapt to the existing systems and procedures that the company has put in place. We Germans are here for that, and we're good at it. If you submit a report on time or two weeks late, you're doing the same amount of work, but if you submit it late, you have to apologize, and that doesn't help you.

"You need to express yourself in a different way instead of constantly apologizing. You need to gain experience with making decisions, being proactive and critical. I don't want a 'yes man' who always tells us what we want to hear. I want you to learn to say *no*. I will be very happy when you say *no* and state your reasons for your position. In your mind, you must change the belief that it's about making a good impression, and this is how coaching is going to help you. Make the best of it. I'm going to give you some important advice that I want you to think about: whenever you make a decision, a decision that is in the interest of the company, nobody is going to throw it back in your face or punish you. Please understand this."

He glanced over and gave the floor to Saskia Süßsauer, Human Resources manager, who was also German. She displayed an on-screen chart with the results of Miguel's evaluation.

"The lowest scores are the ones you gave yourself, where you scored one or two in almost every area, while the evaluations you got from eight other people were much higher. This might be a question of self-esteem. Let's look as some examples: in the part 'solves problems in a flexible and efficient way,' you entered a one, the lowest score, while the others gave you an average of 3.8, with a maximum of five. We get the same thing with 'looks for win-win solutions.' Your best averages are: 'gives people the autonomy to carry out their tasks;' 'he addresses and treats people respectfully;' and 'seeks the best way of satisfying customers' needs.' Your lowest averages are for: 'through team management, he keeps everyone focused on the same objective;' 'effectively coordinates activities within his and other areas;' 'he can prioritize his workload;' 'he stays cool and confident under pressure and when facing difficult issues;' 'talks about problems in an open and transparent manner;' 'balances daily activities with long-term vision;' 'anticipates and facilitates conflict resolution;' and 'encourages people to work as a team.'"

Von Stockelsdorf got to his feet, approached the screen, and said, "When I see this chart, Miguel, the yellow column tells me that your team is really satisfied. Your team feels okay with you. You are a good boss for them. However, if you put that evaluation against your boss's and mine, we get a different picture."

Pointing out the evaluations made by coworkers and bosses, he added, "We need to improve this result. Here is where you can improve. Maybe you won't believe it, Miguel, but you and I are very similar. When I saw these results, it took me back to the first time I had coaching, a long time ago. I had a coach who helped me a lot. More than fifteen years ago. It was the best experience ever. It was very expensive for the company, because my sessions took up my whole day. I had a coach all to myself. That was the greatest personal-development opportunity I've ever had. It was the best investment the company ever made in me. I would not be where I am without that coaching. It was that important.

"I am an engineer, like you. And for me—before coaching—I was not interested in talking nicely with the bosses, but in providing results. In coaching, I learned that I can't get results without the bosses. If nobody takes an interest in my results, they are not worth as much. If I can't have a face-to-face discussion and support my arguments, I cannot grow, because nobody will trust me. And if the others don't trust me, I'm going to do badly. I had to learn how to convince people to follow me. You're already on good ground because your people accept your authority. That's why I'm inviting you to seize this opportunity. We know you can improve your scores. There must be hundreds of people who know who you are, not just those who report to you directly in this period while the company is still small. We are investing in you because it's a great responsibility. And if you don't get ready for this, you are not going to make it."

Saskia looked at the coach and invited her to take the floor.

"Would you please explain to us how this is going to work, so we all understand what's going on?"

"First, I want to tell you, Miguel," said the coach, "that I feel very happy to be working with you. Please, don't hesitate to ask me any questions you have so that you're absolutely clear about what and what not to expect from coaching. Are you okay with that?"

"Yes, sure," he responded.

"The most important thing to make clear is the fact that coaching takes place on two levels. To start with, the company makes a request, we carry out an evaluation, and your bosses outline the developments they hope to see. This is done openly; everyone here knows that you are going to be changing how you do things in order to get the results we want. The second part is the fact that whatever happens between you and me during the sessions is to be treated as confidential. This means that if your boss or Saskia or the director call me for news about you, the first thing I'll do is call you and find out what you would like me to say."

Miguel's expression changed when he heard this. He relaxed slightly into his chair and stared at the coach for a moment. It was like he was daring to see her for the first time.

The coach continued. "You also need to know that only today's session—as it's the beginning—will be held here in the company building. Later, I will let you know the address for the rest of our meetings together. The idea is to let you disconnect from your responsibilities and have some time for yourself. We will have a total of six sessions. We shall also agree upon two periods of observation when I will come and observe you during a work meeting. We will create an Excel file in which you can note your progress, which you will be able to show to your boss as needed. At the end of the process, we will have another session like this one, during which you will present your results and your follow-up plan."

At that moment, Miguel's boss, who until then had been silent, took the floor.

"I want to tell you, Miguel, that we decided to hire the coach for exactly the reasons she just gave. Because of her transparent way of working, I can closely monitor your progress. So from now on, after each session, could you please send me the Excel file she mentioned without my having to ask, so that I can follow up, make recommendations, and ensure you have what you need?"

Then, the boss went over what he had already told him in private.

To prevent them from going on longer and doing everything possible to restrain his impatience, von Stockelsdorf stood up again and slapped the table.

"Very well," he said, "I'm waiting to hear what you have to say about this, Miguel."

"I think I understand better what this is about," Miguel said. "It's an opportunity for me to improve. I'm ready to commit to being better; after all, you are betting on me."

"This is a big day, Miguel. The beautiful sun of Silao is shining on you. Your coach is here. It's Friday. This couldn't be a better time to start. We won't waste any more time. Now Miguel and the coach can talk in peace. We're leaving. Good-bye."

When he passed Miguel, he patted him on the back.

"Good luck," he said, "and may you benefit greatly from this opportunity."

Chapter 9
The Client

It's vitally important for any coaches working in an organizational environment to be fully aware of their client's context as they sit, possibly biting their nails, at the back of the company's meeting room, waiting to be introduced to their coach.

As a first point, we need to state that the nature of the relationship between a coach and his corporate client is complex, due to all the expectations riding on the outcome from the different stakeholders such as the bosses, Human Resources, staff, and colleagues. They all have a stake in the process, directly or indirectly, either as evaluators using the 360-degree assessment (usually done at the beginning and end), as those present when the coach shadows the client in meetings, or as members of teams actively involved in the coaching process. This could equally involve directors and high-level executives as well as production plant managers. Only with this background information can the coach avoid the dangerous oversimplification of approaching the client from an individual's perspective. The approach must be systemic.

> *The individual must be understood as part of the system in which he operates and from the relationships he has with others.*

There is something else we need to look at. Throughout the last fifteen years, the business world has seriously raised its expectations of managers. In the past, it was normal to have specialists in areas of technical expertise in management positions. Their focus was supposed to be on achieving results without caring too much about how. These days they have to demonstrate:

> The dignity of an archbishop, the spirit of a missionary, the perseverance of a tax-collector, the experience of a quality auditor, the working ability of a colossus, the touch of an ambassador, the genius of a Nobel prize, the optimism of a shipwreck survivor, the resourcefulness of a lawyer, the health of an Olympic competitor, the patience of a nanny, the smile of a movie star and the hard skin of a rhinoceros.
> —Friedemann Schulz von Thun

This means that managers today need a broad spectrum of internal resources, which are harder to develop than any technical qualifications obtained with years of training—these are things that don't get taught in school.

The new manager needs to connect with all his potential and creativity to integrate his technical skills with a feeling for people that enables him to understand his own and others' behavior. He also needs to make decisions with a systemic eye and to establish a balance in the activities of the teams working under him. When you add cultural and racial diversity to the mix in global corporations, the challenge grows exponentially. We often come across managers who feel like the "ham in the sandwich" (for a Mexican manager, it would be the "chicken in the taco," as the picture shows Miguel just about to be devoured by his boss) on the point of being pushed by bosses, colleagues, collaborators, and Human Resources, all with conflicting agendas and messages. Add that to the manager's own inner conflict and it can get really serious.

What are some of the motives behind a company offering coaching to one of its executives? Here are some of the missions I have encountered in my own practice:

- to help someone adapt to the new responsibilities of a promotion
- to strengthen leadership
- to improve communication skills
- to better manage conflicts
- to prepare for a position abroad

I have certainly noticed a change in companies that mirrors worldwide trends in the profession of coaching. Several years ago, companies were mainly sending hopeless cases in search of a miracle solution; nowadays, they are demanding more and more coaching for the reason it was originally intended: to maximize a person's potential. This reflects the idea of investing in employees who are seen as assets by the company quite apart from "rescuing" or "healing" employees, which is where the confusion with psychotherapy comes in. When I meet a new client, I am delighted to hear about the company's vision of developing "leaders as coaches".

In the same way that individuals have an inner plurality of voices, organizations also have within a similar multitude, often incoherent and at odds with each other. Once we know how to do inner-team work with individual clients, we can then use the same approach with living teams in the workplace, with the purpose of creating a strategy in which everyone has a place. The difference can be seen in how each member of a team takes responsibility for his own voice, embracing it with a higher level of awareness than he used to. This represents a big improvement to how they each were when literally possessed by their own inner characters.

Chapter 10
The Collapse

As he watched his bosses leave the room, Miguel found himself in the corner, fenced in by the table and the chairs, with vision statements and organizational principles hanging over his head. He needed both arms to lean on the table. The coach locked the door and sat down in front of him, looking direct into his eyes.

"Now we can introduce ourselves in our own way," she said.

He looked at her for a few seconds and then went back to staring into the depths of the table. The sentences that followed allowed him to catch his breath.

She spoke of confidentiality, building trust, openness, and support, and of how she was his ally beyond the expectations and agreements made with his employers. Each statement she made was like a hammer breaking through the blocks in Miguel's mind.

When she asked him what he wished to get from coaching, he replied, "I need your help. I don't know if I am the right person for this job. I am under a lot of pressure and I don't know how much longer I can bear the weight of it. A few months ago, I felt I was at the pinnacle of my career, and now they come to tell me that it's not enough. I'm in a real jam, and I think that it will probably be best if I resign from the company and go and set up shop as a car mechanic; at least then I won't have to continue struggling with the bosses, with the Germans and the people who only increase the pressure on me."

He leaned forward and, like a machine gun, listed everything that was bothering him. When he talked about the pressure of his financial responsibilities toward his sisters and parents, his eyes misted up and a tear ran down his cheek.

To make things clear, Miguel and the coach drew up a relationships map. It looked like this:

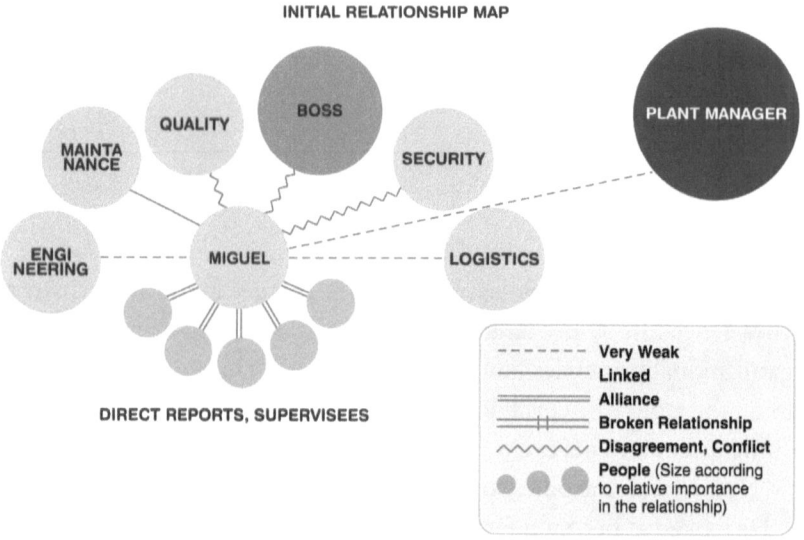

INITIAL RELATIONSHIP MAP

QUALITY

BOSS

PLANT MANAGER

MAINTA NANCE

SECURITY

ENGI NEERING

MIGUEL

LOGISTICS

DIRECT REPORTS, SUPERVISEES

`- - - - - - - -`	**Very Weak**
`————————`	**Linked**
`════════`	**Alliance**
`══╫╫══`	**Broken Relationship**
`∿∿∿∿∿∿`	**Disagreement, Conflict**
● ● ●	**People** (Size according to relative importance in the relationship)

Map interpretation

The coach asked Miguel to assess the importance of each relationship for him in terms of getting results. To the most important, he gave a ten, and the least received one.

These are his evaluations:

- A score of ten for his relationship with his boss. At the same time, he agrees that it's conflictive; it's his biggest red light.
- A score of nine for his relationship with Mauricio in quality, reflecting his importance for Miguel's results. His effectiveness depends on his relationship with Mauricio, and it is with him that he has the highest level of conflict. This is the second vital area of importance to address in the coaching process.
- His main strength is the alliance he has with his team, "his supervisors." Proportionally, the drawing shows a size/power ratio

between him and his team that is equivalent to that of the managers and him. This could indicate that he feels more identification with those under him, for whom he is the "mighty one," and this could explain the conflict he has in his relationships with his peers and his superiors.

- Weak or conflicting relationships with those at the same level, namely, the other managers.
- Weak relationship with the CEO and upper management. This would reinforce the depth of the empathy he feels for those under him.
- The only possible ally that he has on this level is Javier from maintenance; they were coworkers when they used to work together in the same department.

In general terms, this shows that he sees his dependence on others to get the results he needs, which is a real problem for him when the relationships are patchy and inadequate.

"When I look at this, I feel this huge weight on my shoulders," Miguel said. "It's as though all the guys on top are leaning down and crushing me. They're the big guys, and here I am on the five little legs of my loyal supervisors. It's like the little legs can't cope with the weight bearing down on them."

"So, what happens inside you when you realize this?" the coach asked.

"I feel so stressed," he replied. "I understand why I can't sleep at night. I'm like Atlas, with the world on my shoulders. I am pushing against the whole world. That's how I feel. It feels impossible to overcome. I'd have to get rid of all the managers to prove that I can do everything by myself ... you heard Stockelsdorf; he said the managers don't like me."

"I understand that you feel left alone in this situation. And you're saying that you feel it's impossible to overcome this. May I ask a question? Let's just speculate for a moment about what is it that seems impossible for you."

Miguel nodded.

"Imagine that your fairy godmother shows up tonight and, with a wave of her magic wand, she fixes this complex network of relationships. Just like that—everything resolved overnight. When you wake up tomorrow, what would you be doing different?"

Miguel took a deep breath before answering.

"I wouldn't feel as stressed as I do now," he said. "I'd be busy working instead of worrying what others are thinking about me. I'd be working with my supervisors as part of a team. It may be hard work, but I wouldn't be doing it all by myself. I'd know how to plan ahead instead of spending all my time fighting fires and dealing with endless problems. I would have the respect of my boss. The other managers wouldn't be competing with me all the time, looking for ways to put me down in meetings; instead, we would act like members of the same team. I'd speak English and—why not—even German. But here I am, stuck in a trap. I can't go on. It's this crushing weight on me that makes me doubt that I'll be able to stay here."

"Can we agree on something here and now, just between us and in complete confidentiality?"

Miguel nodded.

"Would you be willing to wait until we conclude the coaching before deciding if you're good enough or not for this position? Could you give yourself this time to think about it?"

"Okay, that seems reasonable," he replied.

"Very well. We can play with this idea when you need and decide at the end of the process. Agreed?"

Miguel nodded.

"Now, tell me, have you ever in your life had to deal with something really important that seemed impossible, but that you somehow managed to resolve?

"Many, many times," he said, and he started talking about what it had meant for him to get into high school and what had inspired him to continue on to college in the city. He talked about Damiana, his father, and his dream of being an engineer.

"Which of your inner resources helped you the most to reach your goal?" she asked.

"My voice," he said immediately with conviction and certainty.

"Your voice? How so?"

"Yes, being the soloist and the best singer. Gaining respect. Being superior. Moving up."

"And how today do you use your soloist's voice resource at work?"

"No," he said, looking down. "I don't use it—not here. Here, I shut my mouth. Here, I don't talk. Here, I come to work. Here, they don't even know that I can sing and play the guitar. Here, only my collaborators do what I ask because they know I'm like them and that I managed to get out from under. None of the managers, bosses, or Germans pay me any attention, as you already witnessed.

"They don't pay attention to you. Let me speculate a bit more and ask you a purely hypothetical question: imagine a Miguel whose voice in the company is like that of a soloist, a voice that people pay attention to. How would that person be?"

Miguel remained silent for a while. He took a deep breath.

"It would be … like after the fairy godmother's visit." Big, heavy tears ran down his face and fell on his hand. He did nothing to stop them. "I'd be a leader … with self-esteem … determined … different …"

"Different from whom?"

"From me."

"Would that be possible?" she asked.

"It never occurred to me to even think about it. I'd forgotten that long ago I had a voice …"

Miguel spent a long moment in silence, with his eyes on the table. All at once, he got to his feet, legs slightly apart and feet firmly planted on the ground; he wiped his face and spoke, his voice gaining volume for the first time.

"Here's what I think. I want to carry on working here and do all I can to improve my results. I want to believe that I am here because I can do the job and more. I've overcome much worse situations in life, having nothing to eat and being beaten up and humiliated, so I don't see why I can't succeed at this. But what I want most of all is my voice back. I want my voice to be heard and recognized by the company. My only question is, how?"

Chapter 11
Applying the Model

Friedemann Schulz von Thun was for decades a professor and researcher in the Psychology of Communication Department at the University of Hamburg. His work is considered essential reading in Germany, where his communication model forms the basis for management training and his coaching methodology is widely used.

He states, "I developed the inner team model to make the inner life of a human being something that could be managed and understood, something that could also be used as a way of transforming liabilities into strengths or defects into virtues. By defects, I mean that we are often 'a house divided' in our own lives, where conflicts range from destructive splits to civil wars within ourselves. When I say virtue it is to say that we can use the wisdom and strength of all the different voices belonging to our inner team. With collaborative leadership and the management skills to liaise with each voice, we can transform a group of conflicting personalities into an efficient Inner Team."

The six lessons of the Inner Team, according to Friedemann Schulz von Thun:

1. Inner Plurality

2. Inner Leadership

3. Inner Conflict Management

4. Building Personality

5. Inner Alignment

6. Content of the Situation

1. Inner plurality

As previously stated, we have within us a variety of selves, all of whom have something to say. Some of them agree, and some are in conflict. Generally speaking, they are often disorganized in a similar way to external teams. A key question is: What keeps a team together to ensure that what emerges from this "we" is an authentic, united, and integrated "I" that embraces all our diversity? Each team member contains thoughts, feelings, and needs. But there's more: they also incorporate values, standards, and corresponding commands to the self. So it is useful to imagine that there are a number of "miniature human messengers" within you.

2. Understanding inner leadership

Who is the team leader and what is his function? How does he produce synergy from this inner knot of identities and create a real team? This leader has a tough job caused by the large-scale conflicts that exist among members of the inner team. Leadership is a result of the awareness gained during the coaching process, as the individual learns to manage his inner life and reaches the understanding that each voice or self is just that: part of a whole in which the individual is "stuck" or "frozen" and that by being able to step back and see the whole picture of what's going on, a person can choose the right inner voice to be the leader.

I remember the case of one client, a top Latin American executive whose sense of identity got "stuck" in a character he called "the good boy" who had to obey, remain silent, and never contradict authority. After working with his inner team, he realized that he also had, within himself, an extraordinary negotiator and leader who couldn't emerge because the "good boy" was always in the scorer position.

3. Inner-conflict management

It is well known by coaches that conflicts cannot be avoided and are necessary for our existence, as is the importance of learning to recognize and resolve them. It is necessary to understand the following: How much external conflict can someone resolve, if he himself is undergoing an internal guerrilla war, similar to what we see, for example, in Miguel's case? Which voice will he respond to? Which one will he follow? Which one will step out to oppose the "enemy" out there in his work?

4. Building personality

From the perspective of the inner team model, we can see that not all inner characters show up in the same way:

- There are the "early messengers" and the "late messengers." Early messengers arrive right away and influence the event. Late messengers sometimes only arrive hours or even days later, often with undeniable intensity.
- There are *loud* and *soft* voices. The soft voices are only audible if we pause, stop what we are doing, and switch off the noise.
- There are more or less *welcome* voices. The ones we welcome represent the so-called "primary selves;" these are the parts we strongly identify with and accept because they fit the image of "who I am." But each of our primary selves has an opposing self, hidden underneath the leaves, which is the same size but belongs to our "inner outcasts," the rejected or disowned selves. They represent all that we judge in others.

The fact that some characters are relegated to a spot behind the curtain or hidden in the basement can lead us to mistakenly believe that their voices have less value than that of the lead singer. An inner team cannot be developed unless it integrates both opposing poles. I'll give you an example: a coaching client once yelled at and threatened someone at her office, judging her as incompetent and unreliable. Her leading voice stood behind the judgment. It was someone who could be a "responsible self" who shouted for her; a primary, welcome voice that the client identified with. Many hours later, when trying to sleep, she was swamped with guilt that kept her awake and the consequent terror of getting fired because of her aggressive behavior.

The two voices of fear and guilt appear in her when she is letting go of the day's tensions, as if coming up from the basement. They are therefore "late messengers." They won't leave her alone during the night, but by the next morning, they've been sort of forgotten and "sent to sleep," and the leading role has unconsciously been given back to the "responsible" primary self she identifies with, the one who can fight the daily battles at work.

5. Inner alignment

The lineup of players on a football team depends on the context and situation the team is facing. In this way, our inner lives also develop different lineups. This happens spontaneously and automatically. If we want to change our inner lineup, we need to learn some new skills, namely that it is possible to bring forward our best player depending on a given situation, as well as to send those we don't need "to the bench." Let's think, for example: How do we relate to our mother, boss, or best friend? Being unaware of how our inner selves operate in us, we "bring forward" different "team players" in each relationship and in each situation, showing a pattern of behavior that manifests itself with that particular player. When we apply the inner team model to the coaching process, the client learns to be responsible for choosing the most appropriate lineup for him, especially in complex situations.

6. Content of the situation

The lineup of players in the inner team needs to reflect the situation they face. They all need to be recognized and accepted, each representing a certain polarity. We need to come to an inner agreement among the competing and contrasting energies of all our selves, so that we can communicate  effectively with others. This ensures integrity and congruency. Only when we arrive at an inner agreement are we able to truly "walk the talk" and promote authentic harmony in our communication with others.

The three levels of awareness

Every time you access and then separate from a self, you enter into a process of becoming aware, and you are not the same "you" when you finish the session. You are then free to consciously access another voice for support in a given situation. Becoming aware is actually a process in which you are constantly growing into being the leader of your inner life, instead of being prisoner of the energies and impulses that each self imposes on you.

The three levels of awareness we work with are:

1. The witness state that observes without judging. It doesn't act. It is not attached to the outcome. It realizes something new.
2. In this second level, we separate from the selves we are over-identified with and hold the tension between our polarized selves.
3. About this third level, Hal and Sidra Stone stated: "Someone has to use the gift of awareness and the treasure of experience and, for us, that someone or something was the Aware Ego Process." In other words, we call it "the aware process of becoming a leader of our inner team."

What happens next?

Once we have developed the three levels of awareness, we are then ready to communicate with other people without projecting and judging them. Schulz von Thun defines ideal effective communication as finding a dual agreement within a person's selves and with what that person wants to say. This is achieved by having integrity in this dual-dialogue: the inner dialogue with oneself and the outer one with another person.

"Integrity" in this sense is achieved once we act as leaders being aware, listening and acknowledging the voices of our inner and outer systems.

So, to communicate effectively we need to listen to two sources of information: our multiple selves, and the information and facts of a given situation within a system. Then we need to link and make sense of both kinds of information while communicating.

The coach has a key role in helping the client gain awareness of his inner plurality while making sure that he respects his integrity. He is there to help him observe the system and unveil its implicit rules. In this way, the client can identify, validate, and legitimize his role in that system.

Authenticity and coherence + efficiency = effective communication

Schulz von Thun's model is a significant advance in the psychology of communication, since it integrates and reconciles two major bodies of thought that have been traditionally struggling to dominate our understanding of human behavior:

- Humanism, based on the idea of an individual, autonomous personality striving for self-realization, which has given rise to a series of schools of psychology, philosophy, and communication; and
- The systemic approach and systems therapy, which holds that human beings find their identity by being part of a whole and from the roles and positions they hold within the systems they belong to.

The Schulz quartet

Once we understand that we are made of a number of different voices, we need to direct our attention outward and look at the nature of interpersonal communication on the "frontier," as Bakhtin calls the point where two humans meet—the place where we come into contact with the equally diverse and complex inner life of the "other."

In both of the following instances, we see how pressure is a part of the process. We could call the first moment the "*im*pression," which occurs when something outside of us gets in and the pressure or resistance is generated in its effort to enter our mind (thus leaving an impression). Its arrival leaves a mark, an energy signature, which becomes a voice or character within us. The second part is in the opposite direction, the "*ex*pression," to relieve internal pressure by communicating. Communication with another can only be harmonious if the "expression" is that of the inner team's leader.

After years of research, building on the work of Paul Watzlawick, Schulz von Thun determined the existence not of two but of four messages that are exchanged simultaneously when holding a conversation with another person. He claims that, when a word leaves our mouth, that word is made up of four interlinked voices, creating a harmony that is not noticed by the listener or speaker, even though it is part of "received message."

The message I send, with its four "sub-messages," is frequently interpreted in a different way from what I expected. If, for example, I tell my partner that I cannot go to the cinema while only thinking about the fact of it, my partner may puzzle me by saying, "Of course, that's because I don't mean anything to you. The only thing that means anything to you is your work. You think you're so cool!" Here, we can assume that my partner is hearing a message that reflects on our relationship ("I don't mean anything to you") and on my identity ("You think you're so cool").

These four voices, when mixed up, are at the root of the misunderstandings, biases, disagreements, and impugning of the other's motives that prevent us from accepting others as who they are. They also form the basis for distinct cultural interpretations that are responsible for a kind of blind spot in how we communicate, since most of this gets conveyed in unconscious ways through our pattern of speech, tone of voice, look, speed, bodily presence, feelings, and internal reactions.

The four sides of our communication are:

A) Message content

This refers to the "technical" content or "facts of the matter" being discussed. When you hear people talking in a meeting about "pallets," year plans, or line-stops, these would be the technical contents.

B) Message referring to the speakers' Identity

This is about who I am, based on what I say and how I present myself to the world through my dialogue with you. When I speak, I reveal who I am while talking about anything. Which voice in my inner team is performing the role of "spokesman"? (the big guy, the inferior, always in the right, the critic, the perfectionist etc.)?

C) Message referring to the relationship between both parties

This is about how I view myself with regard to the other. To whom shall I give more power or authority? How do I endorse or discredit the other? What do I want to say about our relationship using my eyes, volume and tone of voice, body language, etc.? From studying effective conflict management, we learn that it is indispensable—especially in those with a risk of conflict—to have agreed on the form the relationship is to take between the two parties first, and to discuss contents afterward. If this principle was understood and thoroughly applied, there would be many organizations that could have saved millions in training, facilitation, and mediation fees. Before implementing a project, do all stakeholders have a clear idea of what is expected of them, what their roles are, how they are going to communicate with each other, and what their part of the bigger picture is?

D) The Intention In the message

In practical terms, this usually means requesting, offering, or proposing some type of action. This would indicate that there is no communication without a purpose, that nothing is said by accident or without a reason.

Every piece of communication involves a request, an agreement, or a need to coordinate with the other; otherwise, there would be no need to address someone with the aim of conversing. Often, that intention might be no more than saying, "I need you to listen to me."

Watzlawick, in his book "Theory of human communication" presented two axioms, the first being that communication is unavoidable, since each and every single behavior is a type of communication. The second is that communication is always intentional. This is how our inner characters sometimes trick us by putting words in our mouths that we will later regret and attempt to justify by saying, "I didn't mean it." Of course it is difficult to accept the harm we have caused when we have offended someone; however, it is important to develop an awareness as to "who" inside us said those words and what message he has for us and the other party.

The coach with four ears and four tongues

So the coach's challenge is learning to listen to these four messages and to question them, like growing "four tongues and four ears," knowing that behind each tongue, there may be several characters from the client's inner life waiting to be discovered.

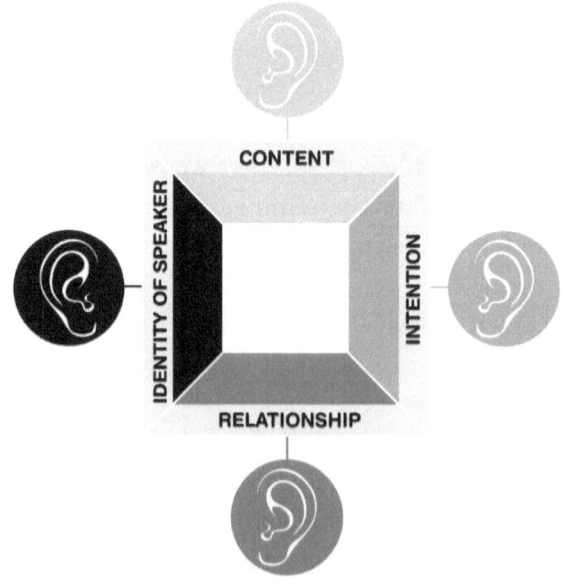

Chapter 12
The Roller Coaster

In all the years of knowing him, Miguel's wife had never experienced anything like this: Miguel came home and talked and talked nonstop for hours, and for the whole evening, he didn't even once try to turn on the TV! *This is amazing!* the woman thought. *I must let him talk.* Miguel was going over what had happened to him, the meeting, the coaching, but he couldn't stop mentioning the soloist voice that he wanted to get back. "I don't know how I kept it silent for so many years," he said. "I feel that I have to make up for the lost time because you're my family, which is why I'm going to make a serious effort to be at home more, to go to the park with the kids and be the dad I always wanted to be."

On the Saturday following his first coaching session, Miguel took his family to Sierra de Lobos and turned off the radio during the trip to tell stories about his childhood, to sing his father's songs and to enjoy their "family time." He played with the children; he played being the soloist, the father and the head of the family.

But, what goes up must come down, and Miguel's great surge of enthusiasm fell flat just as he entered the company gates on Monday morning. His presentation was criticized during the production meeting in front of half the plant. He had to put up with his boss yelling at him in front of all his shop floor collaborators because of an engineering change that hadn't worked. To make things even worse, he called for a meeting with the management to review all the changes his boss was yelling about and only two of them came.

On Tuesday, there was going to be another meeting with the managers and his boss, and the coach was going to observe.

Coach's Notebook

Observation session during a manager's team meeting with the boss
Client :   Miguel
Company : Teile-X
Day :   Tuesday, 10:00 a.m. (after session 1)

Observations

- Quality manager standing at the front of the room. Miguel, at the back, in the dark (missing, blurred); the lights are off.
- Quality manager talks, attacking Miguel (five times in ten minutes).
- Miguel hesitates, stutters, justifies himself, and tries to blame others, or shuts up and passes the slides.
- All eyes are set on the quality manager, although Miguel has the floor.
- Maintenance manager silent, writing.
- Miguel is focused on the computer screen. He doesn't even look up to reply.
- Engineering manager goes in and out of the room five times, using his Blackberry.

- Safety and logistics managers are holding a private conversation, indifferent.
- Boss is silent during the whole meeting; all he does is make notes. He's more conscious of my presence than the others. At the beginning, he said that he did not intend to participate in order to let the managers interact. Every now and then, he turns around and looks at me, pointing out something that he wants me to notice.
- Type of conversations: attack, defense, and counterattack. They just don't want to lose. Each manager defends his turf.
- Tension in the room.
- Miguel's leadership? He is out of sight. He is excluded from view. He is unseen, invisible.
- Feedback for Miguel: change position; take back power over the territory, go where the quality manager is standing now. Delegate the operation of computer. Make eye contact. Facilitate the meeting. Take over the leadership role. He needs to persuade himself and convince me: "I am a manager; I am a leader!"

Warning: I believe it will be an enormous challenge for him to fit in at this level of management, as I notice he has habitual behaviors that are not those of a leader.

Chapter 13
Some Basic Coaching Principles

CONDUCTOR

Most of the issues that demand the services of a coach have to do with conflicts or dilemmas generated because the client needs to make decisions and doesn't know how to proceed. Would it be better to discuss a sensitive topic or to remain silent? Would it be best to dismiss a team member or to tolerate his negativity? Can this person adapt to the new circumstances in the company, or will he continue to resist? Might this be the right time to leave the company and become independent? Will he be able to work any longer with that boss, with whom there's no understanding?

How to keep a cool head instead of exploding when things don't happen the way we want?

To make a properly informed decision, it is important to listen to all the inner voices and examine all the aspects of an issue. That's why this simple and comprehensive list of questions helps the coach.

When is it most useful to involve the inner team in coaching?

1.   When the client needs to know why he behaves a certain way. A client might ask questions such as: Why do I shout at my collaborators, knowing full well that I'm scaring them and that I'll feel

guilty later? Why do I do this over and over again, even when I am committed to improving? Why am I always struck dumb when I'm with the directors and the company's foreign guests?

2. When he needs clarity to deal with a given situation or before taking decisions like those listed above.

3. When he is preparing to address a potentially challenging situation. One example might be a meeting that involves a risk of conflict that he needs to handle effectively.

Once he has heard all the conflicting reasons in his own mind, he has begun to understand himself better. With this new awareness, he will find more effective ways to act.

A lot depends on the context

Something to note about members of our inner team is that they appear in certain contexts, depending upon the person, situation, issue, or challenge.
Some different contexts:

- Daily events of any kind, from the moment the alarm clock goes off, and how the voices react to that: "Shall I get up? Five minutes more?"
- Special events that require us to play a challenging role; for example: a presentation, our own wedding, or a trip to negotiate a major purchase.
- Events that awaken contradictory voices that cannot consent to each other's solutions.
- Decisions on matters where there are conflicting values
- Changes in routine
- Roles where the client is an employer, subordinate, husband, or father. For each role in life, there's an alignment of the inner team that favors certain behaviors (often fraught with conflict).
- Questions about the meaning of life.

Listening to the metaphor

COACH

Using metaphors that have a special meaning for the client can be very useful. A metaphor uses one thing to describe something else. In my years of practice, I have discovered that listening fully to the client is often enough to identify his metaphor. He usually comes up with it himself.

If that person is a soccer (or any other sport) fan, it's quite likely that he will feel comfortable if he uses the "inner soccer team" metaphor and the "lineup" of the players to create a winning team. If dealing with a more intellectual person, it may make more sense for him to use a theater (or cinema) metaphor, with main and secondary characters, etc. If that person is passionate about music, the orchestra metaphor can be used, whether a symphony, mariachi, or a rock band. If dealing with someone who is exclusively focused on his job, what metaphor can be better than the "inner company," one in which there's a director, a human resources manager, or a union leader? For a physician, the hospital metaphor could work, and for those involved in sea and ocean transport, it could be a ship with its captain and crew.

COMMANDER

It is important to stick to the same metaphor used by the client. Don't start playing soccer and then end up with different musical instruments. The coach is at the client's service and needs to practice active listening at all times. For those clients who dislike metaphors, then the work can be done by simply prioritizing the voices coming to the front, whether they are louder or quieter.

Not too long ago, a client set himself the objective of "becoming the ship's captain" in the company's "ship" for his coaching process. I did not need to lead him on this, and, two sessions later, he started exploring his inner voices with hardly any prompting; he used the idea of the ship, captain, and officers when describing his inner characters. There was another client who was describing what was happening to him in the company. While describing something that had been going on, he pointed to his shoulder and said, "So, a little elf climbed onto my shoulder and started saying ..." Later, he added a witch and a dragon to his story.

Chapter 14
Into the Depths

When Miguel came to his second session, he was feeling down again.

"What do you want to achieve today?" the coach asked.

"To at least be able to leave this session the way I did the previous one. Let me tell you that as soon as I got back from our last session, my boss could see the difference. When I got to my post, he started telling me off. 'Hey, why are you late?' he asked me. I told him that I'd been with my coach. 'Ah, yes; sorry,' he said. 'I'd forgotten. It did you some good, eh? I can see that from miles away.'"

"Okay, so to at least be able to leave this session the way you did the previous one. Have you identified an objective you'd like to work on?"

"Yes. I've got three, in fact, but I'll be very happy if I only get one of them done. I want to learn why it is, during meetings with managers and directors, that I remain silent. I also want to know if it's the same thing when my boss yells at me in front of everyone and I bite my tongue."

"Why are you interested in finding out?" the coach asked.

"Well, even though there have been a lot of training courses, several bosses, and lots of advice, I'm still dealing with the same issue and still not able to identify what's behind it."

"Tell me how this fits in with the objectives we set for the coaching process. Is there a link?"

"It has to do with the fact that von Stockelsdorf wants me to be a leaders' leader and wants me to learn to say no to him and my boss. That's the connection. If I don't get to the bottom of this, I won't be respected. What kind of a leader will I be then?"

"How will you know if you have achieved this session's objective?"

"If whatever we discover here can help me speak up when I'm right," Miguel replied.

"And here, with me, what needs to have happened by the time we close the session for you to feel satisfied and walk out as happy as you were at the end of the previous one?"

"If, while I am here, I can figure out what makes me bite my tongue, get free of that, and put together a plan I can use in the meeting tomorrow.

"Excellent. Is it okay with you if we start exploring?" the coached asked.

"Yes."

"I'm going to ask you to imagine yourself back in that meeting like the other day. Take a deep breath and imagine the room and the people there ... now, please, tell me what you see."

"It's the largest meeting room in the company, and it's full of people. Those who can't find a chair are on their feet, leaning against the wall. There are more than thirty people, with quality, maintenance, and the entire production department. I'm at the computer. Before the meeting, I talked to Javier, the maintenance guy, about an important issue that was going to be discussed, and when I told him what I thought, he said he felt the same. That moment gave me some self-confidence. I felt that I was doubly right. However, as usual, the moment the meeting started, the quality guy started in with the long list of all the findings and issues that had turned up during the weekend, and the shooting started."

"What's 'the shooting' like?"

"Everything gets thrown at me and my people. All the things that weren't done right, such as rejects, re-workings, scrap and line stops—those hit the hardest."

"When the quality guy is shooting, can you identify anything that you're telling yourself?"

"Yes, of course. I'm thinking that the bigheaded baby-face is here again with his weekly war, perfect start to a Monday. I hate him. I'd like to kill him. I'd like to scream that it's all lies and that I'm doubly right. I'd like to expose the fact that he does nothing but manipulate information to make it look as if I'm always wrong and he's the little angel. And then I start thinking that I'm useless, that I'm no good at this job, that I have no support, and I start wondering what I am doing here, and my voice weakens."

"Let me see if I follow you. I hear two different messages: on one hand, a voice says that you're not only right, but that you're doubly right. On the other one, a voice hates the quality guy and wants to kill him, while at the same time going after you and claiming you're useless. Am I getting it?" the coach asked.

"Yes, that's it."

"Okay. What else happens in the meeting?"

"Then it's my turn to take the floor, and I start stammering. The Safety guy interrupts me. My boss starts yelling at me in front of everyone. I blush. I have all the answers I need but I remain silent. I feel myself getting smaller. My voice weakens. I lose again."

"And?" prompts the coach.

"Everything gets dumped on me just for a change. I am sick to death of it and know they're going to fire me. Then I think about my sisters and parents and what will happen if I get fired and I know that I really have to defend myself—after all, I am right—and yet, I don't do anything. The truth is that I'm fed up with this happening to me. I spend a lot of time thinking about it and I still don't know what is it that forces me to get smaller in those situations."

"Is it okay with you if we do some more work with these voices and see what we can discover?"

"Yes, of course. I'm extremely interested," said Miguel.

"We'll do an experiment. We will give them bodies and breathe life into them; in fact, we'll do everything possible to know them better, as if they were musicians in an orchestra or members of a football team. Out of the two, which one do you prefer: musicians or a team?"

"Well … let's go with a soccer team, for a change."

"Which voice do you want to start with?"

"With the weakened one."

Voice 1
First Position

The coach took a piece of paper and wrote in large characters: "Weak voice."

"Put it somewhere in the room, somewhere you think it belongs," she said.

Miguel stood up and posted it on the wall to the right.

"Now, stay there, facing the paper, and let your body become like the weakened voice. You can sit or stand, whatever best represents the energy of this voice."

Miguel stayed standing, keeping his back to the wall.

"As long as you occupy that particular spot, you'll be speaking for the weakened voice, not for Miguel, okay?" said the coach while she walked up and stood to Miguel's left. Then she added, "Now take on the physical posture of the weak voice."

After he had done so, she continued. "Hi, there. Thanks for letting me have this conversation with you. So, can you describe what it's like to be this weakened voice living inside of Miguel?"

Looking downward, he said, "My shoulders droop; my knees bend. I'm weak. I can barely breathe." He touched his chest and was quiet for a moment, as if trying to feel his breath. "My body goes all slack. My legs turn to jelly. I couldn't run away if I wanted to."

"How's your energy level?"

"Very low."

"As a member of Miguel's team, describe yourself physically."

"I'm small and thin."

"While you're staring at the floor, what are you thinking about?" the coach asked.

"I want to disappear."

"What is it that you feel most?"

"Fear," he dared to say, after a long pause.

"What kind of situations or places do you show up in?"

"When nothing is certain."

"And with what kind of people?"

"When I am with higher-ups. Yes, I'd never noticed, only when Miguel is in front of people who have authority over him—again," he reflected.

"And how do you show Miguel that you're there?"

"I force him to remain silent," he said slowly, almost whispering.

"Is there some truth or position you are protecting?"

"Mmm ... I am protecting him so that he can survive ... adversity."

"Meaning that if Miguel keeps his mouth shut in front of authority, it is because you are protecting him so that he can survive adversity?"

"Exactly."

"Why do you do this?"

There was a long silence before he answered.

"To survive this," he said, "and the other times Miguel got beaten up. At high school, he suffered … what today is known as … bullying … and …" A big tear ran down his left cheek. "I have never talked about this before …"

He paused.

"What's happening to you?" she asked.

"I'm remembering."

"Is Miguel's current experience in the company like what happened to him in school?"

"Yes … no … no … yes … no, but … not really."

"What's different now?"

"Everything is different. I'm different."

"Well, it's my opinion that you—as a voice—haven't changed at all. Maybe the one who has changed is Miguel, right?"

"Yes, Miguel is different." He inhaled deeply. His eyes dropped back to the floor.

"Let's go back to you as a voice. Can you tell me what your dream is?"

"I dream of all those who attack Miguel disappearing."

"Tell me something: Do you have a name? What's your name?"

"I am 'Weak.'"

THE WEAK

"'Weak.'" She paused. "Is there any behavior that could be taboo for you, something you would never ever do, as 'Weak'?"

"Opening my mouth or defending myself."

"What would happen to you if you opened your mouth?"

"I'd run the risk of being killed or fired."

"Then, what is your role in Miguel's life?"

He took a deep breath. He let the tears run down his face without stopping them. He kept his eyes glued to the floor.

"It is to … help him survive … the blows."

"It would appear that you're protecting him. Your intentions toward Miguel are good."

"Yes. I learned that if Miguel remains silent and listens carefully, I can tell him when he is going to be attacked. If he doesn't react, they go away quicker than if he moves."

"Who is attacking him?"

"In the past, in school, a gang; today—for example—it's the guy from quality."

"And you continue protecting Miguel just like you did before." She paused again. "Tell me, when you are in charge of Miguel, what is he like, and what are the consequences of his behavior?"

"I'd never thought about this before. Well … he becomes weak … he can't get anything done … or hardly anything. Or he does it wrong. Or he does it late and gets reprimanded …" Miguel answered.

"I want to thank you, Weak, for everything you've shared with me. Now, please take a deep breath, and while you're inhaling, feel everything that is happening inside you. Take another breath and feel everything more intensely, and then, when you exhale, expel all that air and all the tension in your body. Fix your eyes on something different, move, give yourself a shake, step out of the character, and let me talk to Miguel again. When you're ready, come back to your seat."

Miguel shook his body, moved his shoulders, and walked. He stretched his neck from side to side and finally sat down facing the coach.

"Take a few moments to just separate from Weak. He remains standing there, while you are now sitting here with me. He is only a part of you. You are you are much more than him."

"This has an enormous depth," he said. "I've never experienced any-thing like this before. It is …" His voice trailed off, and he looked over at the wall to where he had taken on the personality of 'Weak.' "I've never talked about how I got beaten up …"

"So what happens now that you've done it?"

"It sets me free."

"You say that you're a different Miguel today. How did this voice help you become the person you are today?"

"A lot, a whole lot. For example, I am raising my kids so that this never happens to them; although, of course, I've never told them what happened to me."

"Is there anything you'd like to thank this voice for?"

"Yes, thanks to this voice, I learned how to survive."

"And now, today, what do you want to continue using it for?"

"No, I don't want it now; it's no longer useful. It's getting in the way," Miguel replied.

"What is happening to you as you're saying this?"

"I like it. I'm feeling stronger. This is maybe what was blocking me. I had never realized why I was staying silent."

"So you can choose what you want to do with this and the other voices."

"Sure; I know this one can't help me do what I need to do now."

"Great. Let's move on. Do you want to explore the next voice and let Weak sit there for a while?"

"Yes, of course. I want to get to the bottom of this."

"Do you feel like going into the other voice you showed me at the beginning, the one that is enraged, complains, and then attacks you by saying that you're useless?"

"Yes, sure."

Voice 2
Second Position

He got back on his feet and found a spot on the wall, exactly opposite to where the weak voice was located. He wrote: "Black Mask."

"Very good. Please take a deep breath and move to a place and attitude where you think this new voice stands or sits, this voice that talks to you when you're being shot at in the meetings. While inhaling, get in touch with it physically, how it stands, how it feels, and the tension in different parts of the body."

After he had followed the directions, she

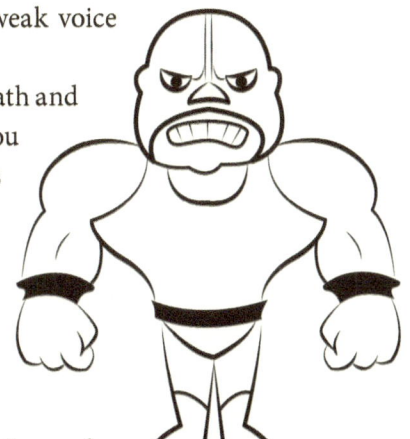

BLACK MASK

said, "So … hi, Black Mask, nice to meet you. Can you tell me what you look like?"

"Hi. Don't you see? I'm big, strong, and very solid. My legs are tense and full of muscles. My arms are the strongest on earth. I wear a black mask so that no one can see me. I have a harsh voice. When I talk, you can hear my voice from half a kilometer away."

"Who are you?"

"I'm Black Mask, the force that destroys everything." He clenched his fist while saying this. His voice sounded sort of childish, as if he'd known this character for a long time.

"My pleasure, Black Mask. Can you tell me what you can see from where you are?"

"I see Weak in front of me. And there's another one," he said, pointing to his right, but without turning to see him. The Conformist.

"Is there a Conformist on the playing field?"

"Yes."

THE CONFORMIST

"Do you want to put down a piece of paper to mark his position?" His posture went rigid. He looked ahead, his right arm pointed firmly toward the Conformist.

"Yes."

The coach gave him the paper, and Black Mask put it on the floor to his right.

"You were saying that you've got your eye on all of them. Who else are you looking at?"

"I'm looking at all those who want to hurt Miguel. I want to attack them."

"Please, could you stand up and look at the one that is the main focus of your attention?"

Black Mask moved to the right and stared at the Conformist.

"I can see that your fists are clenched."

"Yes," he said, clenching them even harder.

"Can you tell me what the message you are sending Miguel is?"

"I tell him 'I told you so! You shouldn't have accepted this; it's useless. How on earth did this idea get into your head?' I have to constantly remind him to keep his feet on the ground and to understand that his dream of being Superman will be his downfall."

"Is it my imagination, or are you mad at someone?"

"Yes, I am—very, because Miguel doesn't pay attention to what I say, and no matter how much I warn him, he continues to do what Weak or the Conformist say," he said while pointing to the wall across the room.

"How do you and your rage show up in Miguel's life?"

"I appear—yes—in the darkness, when Miguel wants to sleep, because he insists on keeping me locked up. I remind him of the foolish things he did during the day. I also appear in his dark thoughts, after he's made a hash of things."

"Is there any other way, apart from the clenched fists, of knowing that you are present? By the way, what happened to your wrist?"

"I broke a glass," he said with a loud laugh. "I did it with the full force of my anger."

"Oh, I see. Sorry, I was asking you, how else do you show up in Miguel's life?"

He took a deep breath.

"It seems to me that ..." He began stammering. The coach noticed his resistance and said, "Relax. This is private. I promise, no one will know about this. Please remember that everything we say is confidential and not even Miguel can hear."

"Thanks. In that case, and only because it's confidential, I can admit ... that I'm ... vindictive and vengeful," he said in a halting voice. "Black-hearted."

"And how do you get revenge?"

"I criticize those who make Miguel look bad."

"Who do you criticize them in front of?"

"In front of his team and with the people from the shop floor and the production line. Can I be sure you won't tell?"

"One hundred percent sure."

"And then, on purpose, I make Miguel neglect things that will hurt quality and their results, or I do something to make things difficult for his boss, who thinks he has the right to treat Miguel like trash. This is how I get back at them for the things they do to Miguel. The truth is that I don't do anything serious enough to attract attention. It's all hidden. But deep down inside, I enjoy my revenge, how sweet it is."

"Are you protecting a value or an important position when you do that?

"Justice. I'm making up for all the bad things done to Miguel, and I protect him."

"So, you protect him?"

"Yes, but as I am not getting through to him, I have to shake and belittle him in the hope that one of these days, he'll listen to me."

"So, what is your deepest wish as Black Mask?"

"I want to wipe them out, so that I can finally see justice done. If I wipe them out, at least in fantasy, Miguel might listen to me for once in his life."

"Who do you want to wipe out?"

"Those two," he said, pointing at Weak and the Conformist, "and the others who attack Miguel."

"Are they easy to wipe out?"

"No, because Miguel pays too much attention to them."

"It looks like you two are really messing with Miguel's head."

Black Mask burst out laughing.

"I don't give him much peace," he said. "Just look at him."

"Tell me something here, just between us: Now that Miguel has decided to take a walk, how do you get revenge against him?"

"Against Miguel? Me? That's some question you're asking!"

"Yeah, that's my style—inquisitive, you might say ..."

"My revenge against Miguel ... how ... well." He looked at the coach with bright eyes and a big, sarcastic smile. "I'll tell you. I make him suffer. I make him feel guilty; I make his stomach hurt."

"So?"

"I give him a stomachache, a headache, and pains for being so useless and such a 'hopeless case.' And what I enjoy most is making him suffer even more at night, when he's defenseless and just wants to sleep. Sometimes he chokes and feels as though he can't breathe anymore with all that goes through his head."

"And that's amusing for you, I can see."

"Yes. He should have listened to me a long time ago."

"What about?"

"I always told him that his thing was music, not engineering."

"Who do you sound like, Black Mask, with such words?"

He swallowed before answering.

"Like his father," he said and sighed in amazement. "I'd never thought of this."

"So you show him every day that engineering is not his thing?"

"I won't forgive him."

"Tell me something. Is there any taboo or behavior within you as Black Mask that you cannot deal with, some sort of 'kryptonite' that would destroy you?"

"You and your questions. I'm the bad guy, the vengeful one; what could possibly kill me? Maybe ... if one day ... Miguel was to experience ... joy! Yes, if he started enjoying life, that might finish me off. Yes, if my words could no longer make him suffer and he started enjoying his work as an engineer. If he started to enjoy being with his wife and children. That could hurt me."

"Enjoy. How interesting!"

Miguel began to move. His legs bent. He leaned against the wall.

"What's happening, Black Mask?" the coach asked.

"I don't know. I got tired."

"You got tired. Anything else?"

"What I said wiped me out," Miguel replied.

"Do you want to take a break?"

"Yes."

"Black Mask, thank you very much for taking the time to talk. Please inhale deeply and highlight all the sensations and tension in your body caused by this self, and then exhale. Now take another breath and, as you exhale, release everything in a single blow, shake yourself, take a step forward, and move your body. When you're ready, you can return to your place."

Third Position
Realization

Miguel needed to run some water over his face before moving on with the session.

"First, sit here and take a moment to separate from Black Mask. He is over there and he is only a part of you; you are much more than him. Take a deep breath and just sense him as separate from you. So, what is coming to the surface in your mind?" the coach asked.

"I discovered another self: 'Distressed.'"   **THE DISTRESSED**

"Shall we make a piece of paper for him?"

Miguel was already doing it. He put it down on the floor, near the Conformist.

"Anything else?" the coach asked.

"Too many things. I have a guy with a black mask living inside my chest, who I had no idea existed, and he looks like my father. It's sort of scary to realize how mean I can be and the damage I inflict on myself. But worst of all is that I live in constant pain and can't enjoy anything. It's true that I don't enjoy anything. So what's going to happen to me if I go on like this, suffering, complaining, and carrying this terrible weight? It's so hard ... so heavy ..."

"So?"

"So there's something else I just noticed. It's to do with 'Distressed.' I spend the whole day micromanaging the results that are handled by my team's coordinator. And I'm constantly all over him, asking how he is doing, if the week's plan is ready, if he has done the statistics. I live in a state of permanent anguish thinking about those results. And now that I come to think of it, in the two years he's been with me, how many times has he goofed off? Zero! He hasn't let me down once. But I continue to get in a state over this, and whenever I go near him, he ducks down because I am all over him. It's shocking. I'm completely stressed for no reason at all. This will give me the opportunity to leave him alone so he can get on with his job, and I'll be able to do something useful with my time," Miguel explained.

"I'm glad that you're becoming aware of all these things. In order to finish this, we need to take a final step. Do you still have some energy left?"

"Sure, I'm with you to the finish line. I said I wanted to get to the bottom of all this."

Fourth Position
The Strategic Observer on the Balcony

"Very well. For the last step, we need to go to the other end of the room from where we can have a full view of everything that's going on."

Pulling up two chairs, the coach asked Miguel to stand on one of them while she got up on the other.

"It's from here that you take the form of your team's director, the one who will lead the team members out on the soccer field," said the coach, pointing at the wall and the floor. She also pointed toward the two chairs they had just left before taking up their new and elevated positions, and she said, "Imagine you're still sitting there with your coach during your session. At this moment, you can see better than any of them. Do you follow?"

"Yes, yes. Now I get to manage the whole game: both Miguel sitting down here with his conflicts and the players on the field."

"Exactly. Now *you* are the team leader, and you decide where they go and what they do. This means that from now on, there's no reason to let them possess Miguel, and it's you who decides when they go into action. You can bring more players on if you think it will help. You can also decide to bench any player who isn't working out in a certain situation. In other words, you—as the leader—get to decide what they do and how they influence your life. How does this sound to you?"

"Great, what a relief. And yes, of course I want to change all this."

Quickly, the team leader headed toward the selves. He marked out an area like a soccer field and selected the right side to serve as a forward area. He picked up the pieces of paper, taking Weak, Distressed, and Black Mask off the field.

"These three can stay on the bench," he said. Then, he took some more paper and started writing without saying a word. Later on, he laid his strategy out on the floor:

"If Miguel keeps playing Weak in the game with his colleagues in management, he will never get their respect. If he leaves Distressed as team leader, he'll never be able to rely on them or do anything useful. If he lets Black Mask continue to harass him every night, he'll end up destroying Miguel by making him ill. If I add the desire to please those in authority, he won't resolve anything, and Miguel will keep putting players into the field who aren't up to the job."

"So, what's your new team like?"

"I need to bring in the Soloist; the one who used to sing when Miguel was young. Not to have him playing solo, but because he can face the most demanding audience and because everyone admires him. That's why he's the Scoring Soloist."

"How do you visualize the entry of the Scoring Soloist onto the field? Describe to me what this looks like in real life."

"The Scoring Soloist enters with a firm tread. A big audience does not scare him at all. Quite the opposite, it's what he likes best. His information is up to date, and he has all he needs to make decisions. The Scoring Soloist is a fully experienced manager who doesn't mind when people try to knock him down. He knows how to defend himself and has everything under control without losing his cool—just like the Germans, who are masters of this art."

"How do you feel now that the Scoring Soloist has entered the scene?"

"Relieved. He's the one Miguel needs," he replied.

"So where else could he be useful?"

"To set limits with the boss and help Miguel move up to divisional manager—like von Stockelsdorf expects. He can help him at home, too. The Soloist knows deep down what Miguel needs, right?"

"You are the leader. You know best what is best for him!"

"Right!"

"And those behind the Soloist?"

"The Scoring Soloist cannot and should not play all by himself. Someone has to pass the ball to him. He won't be able to score unless he is self-confident, and that's why he needs to receive the ball from Doubly Right. Doubly Right is important, although he can be stubborn if you don't watch him; for this, we need one in center field who can weigh things up. To do that, I will need to know what's going on around me."

"When you look at this move, what goes on inside you?"

"It's a winner's move, exactly what Miguel needs."

"Then let's go back to your initial position." They both sat down again. "First, take a deep breath and get in touch with the strategic leader of your team, who is standing right behind you. As one of your team members, you know how crucial his role is for you. Now, take a good look at the new team lineup that he has created, and be aware of how this feels to you.

"What are the concrete steps that you will be able to take if you choose this new strategy?" she asked.

"What steps will I be able to take? It's everything I'm striving for. The first would be to talk to my boss and ask him to stop yelling at me in public. Two: I need the production-line reports on time to get organized for the Monday meetings. Three: I'll stop complaining, because if I complain, I'll lose touch with the Scoring Soloist in the forward line. Four: I'll start working with my coordinator as soon as I get back to the office. The month closes today, and instead of micromanaging him, I am going to let him do his job, just like he has always done. It's quite embarrassing to admit this. Poor guy! He has put up with me for such a long time. I'll sit down with him to help figure out what the priorities are and prove that I trust him. He needs to know that I trust him. I feel something inside is flowing and taking away a lot of anxiety, just as I speak."

"Judging by the self-assurance in your speech now, I don't have the slightest doubt that you will quickly follow through on all four of these points."

"All that means is I can go home early and rest. At home, the Scoring Soloist has to get in shape again. In the evening, when the kids have gone to bed, I'll go to the gym and get back to my old workout routine. It was so well known in my neighborhood that a lot of people copied it," said Miguel.

"Terrific! Is there anything I can do to support you?"

"Issues will come up, for sure, but for now, you've already done a lot. I'll use the company's reporting tool for giving feedback and talk to the boss, and I will request information from the supervisors without allowing any room for failure."

"What has changed in you, Miguel? You are talking to me with a different tone and looking me in the eye! Do you realize that you used to not look at me, and now you do?" she asked him.

"I feel that I no longer have a millstone round my neck. I feel liberated. It's very strange, as if I had really lost weight. I believe the big difference is that now I know I am in control of what happens to me. Yes, that's it."

"When the session began, you had a question you wanted an answer to during this session. Did you get an answer?"

"Well, I think we went much deeper and way beyond my objective. It's going to take me some time to integrate everything I saw today. I don't feel as happy and euphoric as I did after the previous session, but I do feel I'm seeing things clearly now. I have much more clarity. That's what I'm taking with me," he responded.

"Are you taking your players with you?"

"They're right here!"

Miguel and the coach stood up. He picked the pieces of paper up from the floor and tucked them into his notebook.

Chapter 15
Recognizing and Naming Each Voice

Recognizing the voices

Our first task is to identify the "selves" within the client who show up in a given context, event, or situation.

Possible questions:

- In your mind, what do you tell yourself when you think about this situation?
- Describe your inner dialogue when you think about this.
- What do you tell yourself when you hear yourself speaking?
- Is there anything else you tell yourself, other than what you have already mentioned?

It is important to listen for how the messages relate to each other and link those coming from different voices within the flow of dialogue.

For example: "On one hand, I believe that I'm the one who creates the best sales strategies for the company and that I'm very creative. On the other hand, when directors are present in meetings, I remain silent and wait for others to speak because I feel that my contribution is not as valuable as theirs."

In this paragraph, we can identify two types of voice. The first one is conveying this message: "I create the best strategies and I am very creative," while the second one says: "What I have is not as valuable as what they have." Evidently, these are contradictory voices, in conflict with each other, and they show up under different circumstances. The client hears the first one when he is by himself and the second one when he is in a meeting with his bosses.

The selves are "pure" and feature a single energy, or a single attitude toward life. It is of key importance to avoid mixing up the client's identity with those of his voices—especially when they are "unspeakable" or rejected and often bring in an inner critic so as not to "look too bad."

For example: a client, when personifying her "envious self," begins to describe all the things she envies in an intelligent and pretty colleague who is also popular among men, and then suddenly, she comes out with: "Well, I don't only envy her and start gossip, I also say good things about her and recognize her virtues." Here it is not the envious self who intervenes, but another voice who probably feels guilty when she hears herself admitting that she's envious.

There's a key that I find useful to distinguish the voices as they appear during the coaching process, and that is to think of them as if they were selfs in a fairy tale. The witch is only the witch, and she's bad; there's no place for kindness in her. The princess is only the princess. The rebel only knows how to rebel, and the gentle hero has only good qualities.

Naming each self

If we find ourselves working with a client who finds it difficult to get in touch with his inner voices, we might suggest he "look" at some of the following ones, identified by Hal and Sidra Stone (after decades of work with thousands of persons in many different countries). These are the ones that appear more frequently—to varying degrees—in nearly every human being. The name, impact, or message content may differ, but the self outlines can often resemble those described below.

The first thing to know, once the first voice has been named and identified, is that it will have an opposite. Thus, *perfectionist* corresponds to *imperfect*, *hard worker* to *lazy*, and *Mother Teresa* to *selfish*. These opposing voices are the ones we are not willing to accept; we reject them because they go against the image we have of ourselves. In my country, Mexico, we are often used to hearing psychologists saying, "If it strikes, there's a match." In other words, what you find irritating and annoying in others represents a part of yourself that you find irritating and annoying and one that you'd rather not look at.

Another thing to note is that the voices appear grouped in a way that reflects each individual's personal style, like "crews" working together as champions of our stability and security.

1) The "inner critic"

In the book with this same title (*The Inner Critic*), Hal and Sidra Stone explain the origin of this self who lives in all of us by telling the first part of *The Snow Queen* by Hans Christian Andersen. When I re-read it, after many, many years, I felt the same fear I'd felt when I read it as a girl.

> Now then, let us begin. When we are at the end of the story, we shall know more than we know now. So to begin.
>
> Once upon a time there was a wicked sprite; indeed he was the most mischievous of all sprites. One day he was in a very good mood, for he had made a mirror with the power to cause all that was good and beautiful when reflected within to look poor and mean while everything that was worthless and ugly was shown larger and uglier ... Even the loveliest landscapes appeared like boiled spinach, and the people became hideous, and looked as if they stood on their heads and had no bodies. Their faces were so distorted that no one could recognize them, and even one freckle on a face appeared to spread over the whole of the nose and mouth. "This is great fun!" said the sprite. If a good thought passed through a man's mind, then it was misrepresented in the mirror, and the sprite laughed heartily at his cunning invention. All the little sprites who went to his school—for he kept a sprite school—told each other that a miracle had happened and declared that people could now, for the first time, see what the world and mankind were really like. They carried the glass about everywhere, till at last there was neither a country nor a people who had not been looked at through this distorted

mirror. They even wanted to fly with it up to heaven to see the angels, but the higher they flew the more slippery the glass became, and they could scarcely hold it, till at last it slipped from their hands, fell to the earth and was broken into millions of pieces. And now it worked much more evil than before, for some of these pieces were no bigger than a grain of sand, and they flew all around the world. When they got into a person's eyes, they lodged there and from that moment everything he saw was distorted or he could only see the worst side of what he looked at. Even the smallest fragment retained the same power as the whole mirror. A few people got a fragment of the looking-glass in their hearts which was terrible, for their hearts became cold like a lump of ice. A few of the pieces were so large that they could be used as window-panes through which one could no longer see one's friends. Other pieces were made into spectacles which were dreadful for those who wore them, for they could see neither well nor correctly. At all this the wicked demon laughed till his sides shook—it tickled him so to see the mischief he had made as the fine splinters flew about in the air ... [9]

When someone is looking through the lens of the inner critic, the first thing he hears is: "You're wrong and they're wrong." It's the voice that is constantly judging our actions. It's the voice that, no matter how hard we try or how successful we are, judges us more and more harshly. It's the voice that stops us in our tracks as we are growing and moving forward in life. It shuts down our creativity. It makes the smallest ordinary mistake seem like a crime against humanity. It's the voice that criticizes us before others do and is can be heard in phrases like: "you're wrong;" "you're fat and worthless;" "you're old;" "you have no talent;" "you're useless;" "you're boring;" "you'll never amount to anything;" "you're defective;" and "you're an impostor." But, above all: "you don't deserve it."

Thanks to the profound work done by Hal and Sidra Stone with the

---

[9] Andersen:, *The Snow Queen.*

"inner critic," we can see two separate lines of attack. The first is the "fault-finder," always focused on looking at others from a twisted perspective and never satisfied in its constant search for defects or imperfections that it can judge, mock, put down, or reject. With the second line of attack, it implacably turns its all-criticizing eye in our own direction, attacking and destroying us inwardly, while the sprite of Andersen's tale shrieks with laughter.

On this, I'd like to share an experience I had while writing this book. As I went deeply into this material, I found myself locked into an introspective state while discovering what it meant for me personally, (I cannot detach myself or remain intellectually aloof when working with this), and I had the following dream:

> I was with my older son, running down the streets of my childhood, seeking refuge in the neighboring houses, because my sister "Jiminy Cricket" was chasing us and firing a shotgun ... aiming to kill! We needed to find protection to survive the attack.

When I woke up, I burst out laughing. I was dreaming about my inner critic! The one who was bombarding me with criticisms about my own capacity to write a book, my first book, was represented in the dream by my first child. Thanks to this, instead of feeling disturbed by this dream of being hunted by someone as close to me as my sister is in real life, the message of my inner voices became crystal clear: "you're attacking yourself so that this first book dies and never sees the light." Realizing this made it possible to include Jiminy Cricket's criticism and to carry on writing in a relaxed and happy state of mind.

Now, I am not trying to upset anyone. This is not about playing amateur psychologist or doing Jung's, the psychoanalyst's, or anyone else's work for them. I want to use this example to show that some of our inner selves appear in our dreams, in the form of someone we know. The mystery is not in asking why such a person appeared in the dream, but rather which of my inner voices has chosen to appear and assume their identity. Let's be clear. I am not suggesting dream analysis in a coaching session, by any means. I simply want to draw attention to the fact that, as human beings, we have this wonderful resource, and that it can be an avenue of exploration if anyone is as curious about this stuff as I am. While on the subject, I'd like to add that personally, I find that Jung's approach has the most to recommend it.

2) "The pleaser"

He's the one who always wants to be nice and well thought of, to be the good boy. He wants to make others happy. He puts others' needs above his own and can get overwhelmed by work because he can't say no. His need for harmony prevents him from saying anything that might rock the boat or risk conflict. There are people who have a huge "pleaser" that is very active in their lives; they are conspicuous for their inability to say no and for an almost knee-jerk reluctance to get involved in any type of disagreement, confrontation, or difference of opinion with others.

In my experience with managers and directors in different cultures, I have observed that this self occupies a larger inner part of individuals from cultures who suffered the process of colonization in Latin America than in Europeans or North Americans. The over-identification with this self creates a lot of conflict at work. When the "pleaser" is too strong, the individual forgets to focus on results and is too oriented toward saving face with others, "being friends" with his staff and adopting a submissive attitude before authority. This results in poor performance and an inability to guide teams or maintain discipline.

In the Riemann-Thomann model, the pleaser is located at the polarity of closeness and permanence, as we saw in Chapter 7.

3) The "pusher"

This voice exhorts us to get going, to do more, faster and better; he's never satisfied and is always raising the bar. If this self has too much influence, we can turn into "race horses" always in pursuit of an objective that we will never achieve. This voice demands recognition. He wants our lives to be a success. It's the voice of ambition. The one that takes us to a book-store to buy a lot of books on subjects we'd love to learn about, until the "inner critic" shows up and berates us for not reading enough, not reading thoroughly, for forgetting what we read or for not being able—as others are—to quote the sayings or thoughts that have inspired us. The "inner critic" works with the "pusher" to tell us: "look at them, they're way ahead of you."

The "pusher" is restless. He has enormous energy and a relentless capacity for action. No one is as fast, effective, or charming as he is.

In the Riemann-Thomann polarity model, he belongs to the group of selves that bring together distance and change.

4) The "perfectionist"

This is another inner self that helps us to achieve success. He wants us to look perfect, act perfectly, and be perfect in everything we do. He will not tolerate sloppy work. The perfectionist sets the standards of perfection. So if our target is perfection, then whose job will it be to make sure we clearly see all our imperfections? Of course, our friend, the inner critic.

The perfectionist is rigid and judgmental; he generalizes a lot and holds himself up as the benchmark against which the world must be measured. Nobody has the slightest chance of meeting the demands or expectations he puts on them. This is demonstrated in the case of the son who proudly shows his final grades to his father, achieving one hundred in every subject, except one for which he got an eighty. The perfectionist father, looking at the results, says nothing about the ones where he got a one hundred and asks him: "How come you only got eighty? Eighty is the number of mediocrity."

In the Riemann-Thomann polarity matrix, this corresponds to distance and permanence.

General features of our selves

1. The protector

The protector is whom we identify with when we proudly say, "That's the way I am." It's the voice that acts like a permanent radar system, ready to respond, attack, flee, or keep us frozen in case of threat. The one we have next to our skin.

2. The quick and the slow voices

The quick ones are those that appear spontaneously and are quick to jump in and get involved in events. The slow ones appear after a few hours or days and often attack ferociously. Those are the ones that will not let us sleep after something we've said or done, or that appear in our dreams—as it did in mine, with "Jiminy Cricket."

3. The loud and the soft voices

We can only hear the softer ones when we stop moving, uncouple ourselves from the action, and listen carefully. They are so soft, sometimes, that they appear only as a vague sensation or impulse.

4. Owned and disowned selves

Disowned voices are embarrassing, and we would get rid of them if we could. However, the fact is that our self-acceptance hinges on our learning to welcome those unpleasant voices. Where do the unwanted voices go? They come in through the back door and speak to us through the body, as symptoms (headache, gastritis, anxiety, etc.), or in our dreams.

5. The voices are linked to each other.

They are in touch with each other; they converse. They are related and work as a team. Depending on what's going on with us, we will feel better or worse; we use our strength to resolve inner relationships or act vigorously in the outside world.

Chapter 16
Behind the Curtain

"Coach?"

"Yes."

"Hello, this is Miguel's boss."

"Oh, good to hear from you. What can I do for you?"

"I want to tell you something. Miguel came and spoke to me today, and I'm wondering if it's something to do with the coaching."

"I'm listening," the coach replied.

"He came and told me that when I reprimand him in public—he said that I yell at him; the truth is ... well ... that's an exaggeration, and it's not true. I don't yell at him. I just raise my voice a little, but that's because he makes me crazy, you know? Anyway, he came to tell me that he doesn't like it when I tell him off in public and that when I do it, he feels humiliated and angry. He says it destroys his motivation to work. He says I undermine his authority in front of his people, and that if I have feedback for him, could I give it to him in private. What I want to ask

you is—does this have anything to do with the coaching? Did you send him to talk to me?"

"No, I didn't send him. So how did his message 'land' with you?"

"I was stunned. That's the last thing I expected of him. He's a quiet type; he wouldn't say boo to a goose," he replied.

"So, did you manage to come to some agreement?"

"Yes, and I don't know how it happened. I gave him my word I wouldn't do it again. I can't figure it out; not only that, but I also promised that I would speak well of him. He wants it known that he is my right arm and that there is no war between us. I'm really surprised. I don't know how he came out with it."

"So?"

"Well, I mean, I don't know what's going on with him. It's like he's been possessed by someone else. It's very weird. What's true is that he has completely changed overnight, and I really wasn't expecting that."

"I remember that Stockelsdorf insisted that Miguel learn to say no—"

"Yes, but I never imagined he would start with me!" he said and burst out laughing.

"So now that you are seeing this, where does that put you, as his leader?"

"Well … judging by the serious way he addressed me, I see that things are going to have to change. First, I want to see if this really comes from within him or just because Miguel is doing some coaching with you; to be honest with you, he often drives me up the wall."

"Now that he has managed to have this particular conversation with you, do you think you can give him the benefit of doubt?" the coach asked.

"Yes, of course. Definitely. I just wanted to share this with you."

"Thank you very much. As we agreed, you and I are going to have a follow-up conversation later. Let me know if you want to hold it sooner, okay?"

"Yes, sure. Well, that was all I wanted to say. Thank you very much."

"Good-bye."

From: miguel.hernandez@teile-x.com
To: coach@gmail.com
CC:
Subject: BREAKING NEWS

Hello, Coach!

Here is an update: Last Friday, I went to my boss's office and talked to him. I asked him never to yell at me in public again. I don't think he was expecting that, and he went all serious. I told him everything I feel when he yells at me and puts me down. I felt a lot happier than I have for a long time. For the first time in all my years with the company, I let it all out. I was even driven to tears of rage but I didn't feel embarrassed.

However the big news is that this morning, during the Production meeting, with everyone there as usual, he stood up and apologized to me in public! He said a lot of good things about me. He acknowledged me in front everyone and apologized for losing his temper. He said he gets mad at me because Production is his lifeblood, but that he has nothing personal against me. Everyone is talking about it in the company. I can't believe it. I needed to tell you. This was a winning entrance for the Scoring Soloist!

Best regards,
Mit freundlichen Grüßen/Saludos
Miguel Hernández

Chapter 17
Exploring Each Self

To do this, we need to keep in mind the fact that communication among inner team members will reflect the communication we have in our relationships with others. Therefore, we look for:

A. A snapshot of his *identity*. Who is he among the others? What's he like? Is he energetic? What about his body posture? What is his general attitude?

B. Their vision of life, coming through what they say and their *messages,* as each team member has his own perception and defends his position based on his values.

C. In the way they establish their relationships, we learn how they deal with the other inner team members and what their positions are on the "field" (inner alignment). We get to know what they think of each other, and how the "team leader" deals with other individuals, if a certain inner player has been put in command.

D. Through their intentions, they share what moves them and how they operate, to whom they address their messages (perhaps the team leader, another team member, or an external third party), and whether they have something in mind, a request, a proposal, a demand, or a suggestion that they want the rest of the players or the "technical director" to hear.

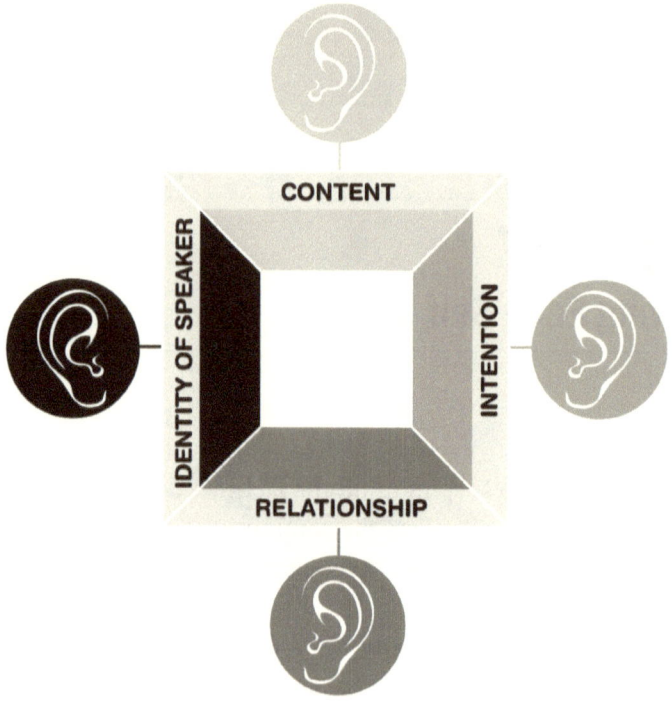

Once we have identified at least two voices, their messages, and the other members of the inner team, the next step is getting to know each player better by using the Schulz Quartet (discussed in Chapter 11).

Among the primary selves, we need to identify the one that is loudest and closest to the client, the voice with which he identifies himself. The protector. Then, we can start exploring that voice. The client is asked to change seats, so that he can take the place of that self. During the process, the client has to report (in the first person) everything this self says about himself, his relationship with the rest of the team members, his purpose or intention, and what he wants from the "director"—that is to say, the client.

You can also put pieces of paper on the floor with the names of each inner team member and ask the client to take up the role of each one of them. Or simply do a drawing and ask him go round the page and talk as each team member would. In this process, there's no limit to the coach's creativity.

Here are some of the questions that might get asked:

A. **Identity**
   a. What are you like physically? Describe your posture, your eyes, your voice, your tone, your breathing? Adopt that posture during the whole conversation with this self or team member.
   b. How do you see yourself?
   c. How are your energy and activity levels? Low or high? Warm or cold? Close or distant?
   d. What do you believe about yourself?
   e. How are you feeling right now? How do you normally feel?
   f. You, as (client's) team member, what do you dream of? What's your main fantasy?
   g. Do you have a name?

B. **Message**
   a. What are you defending in (client's) life?
   b. What kind of things do you say?
   c. What are your principal values?
   d. When and how do you show up in (client's) life?
   e. In what contexts are you more active?
   f. What do you want to say about this particular issue that brought you here today?

C. **Relationships**
   a. What do you think of the rest of the team members?
   b. Who are you, in relation to the rest of (client's) inner team?
   c. How do you get on with the other team members? Do you have any inner allies or enemies?
   d. How do you get on with the "director" (client)?
   e. How does your "director" relate to others when you are in charge?

D. **Intention/purpose**
   a. When you act as you do in front of others, what do you do it for?
   b. What do you expect to get from others?

    c. If your "director" was listening to you right now, what would you ask him for?

    d. What is it that you protect him from?

    e. What do you have to offer him in this particular situation?

Chapter 18
Miguel in Motion

"I found someone else, another inner voice," Miguel said at the beginning of the third session.

"So, tell me about him."

"He's one who doesn't know how to say no, one who'll do whatever it takes to make others happy."

"What else?"

"He's attentive and wants to help. He likes smiling. He is optimistic and likes everyone around him to feel happy. He's a good friend of Weak and he calls in Distressed. His attitude is, 'I am here to fulfill your wishes; ask me to jump and I'll say, how high? Just tell me what you want. I'm your devoted servant and will do anything you ask.'"

"How interesting! What's his position on the inner soccer field?"

"He plays midfield."

"In what context does he appear?"

"For example, when I want them to notice how I'm always willing to take on even the most complicated task or the ones no one else wants, like working weekends. 'Yes, boss, I'll do it;' 'Yes, supervisors, I know how to do that;' 'Yes, Mom, I'll pay for Lucila's school;' 'Yes, Dad, I'll buy you a new guitar;' 'Yes, wife, I'll take out the garbage;' 'Yes, neighbor, I'll help you with your broken-down car;' 'Yes, Miguelito, I'll play trains with you;' 'Yes, for next week;' 'For the day before yesterday, yes;' 'For Germany, yes;' 'For the new project, yes.'"

"I see that with every yes, your chest keeps expanding, as if you were proud of yourself and your ability to take on all these things."

"I feel powerful when the Pleaser is in charge."

"He's got a name."

"Yes, and a motto: 'your wish is my command.'"

"What else can he do?"

"He gets along well with everyone. Does everything he is asked and only wants to do good for others. I can pick up on the slightest hints, and I feel happy when I can read someone's mind and know to please them. I am the most devoted member of the team." He smiles when saying this. "I am the opposite of Black Mask, of course.

"And you're even talking in the first person. Had you realized that?"

"No. How?"

"First, you talked about the Pleaser as a self that 'gets along with others.' Then, you said 'I can pick up on the slightest hints and I feel happy when I can read someone's mind—"

"True!" He burst out laughing. "He's really a part of me, more than any other in the team."

"It's good that you can see that. And what is the Pleaser's dream?"

"His dream is to become the most indispensable person in the company, the guy that can work anywhere in the plant, because nobody knows the guts of the operation the way he does, and there's no one more committed than he is. His kryptonite is, obviously, saying no; if he said that, he wouldn't be the Pleaser anymore, he'd be the Selfish—"

"What would happen to the Pleaser if he said no?"

"Mmmm ... Stockelsdorf would be delighted," he said, laughing again.

"He amuses you."

"Yes. Something about the voices is fun and serious at the same time. Here's how it goes: the Pleaser comes and says yes to everyone, so Distressed appears, feeling wretched and wringing his hands because he has no idea how the hell he's going to honor so many promises. And do you know what I've figured out? That what appears good isn't always. What I think is the best of my selves is actually the worst. So anyway, I wanted to tell you that I've added another player to the game."

"Who's that?"

"The one who firmly and respectfully says no—without guilt!"

"And his name is ..."

"Mr. No."

Follow up on the action plan of:
Miguel Antonio Hernández

Follow-up session
Attended:
Boss, Coach, Miguel

Stage in the process:
Three sessions completed (three left)

Location:
"South Pacific" Meeting Room

Date:
Wednesday, 5:00 p.m.

Miguel Hernandez Coaching Follow-up

*Objective :
- To become the leaders' leader

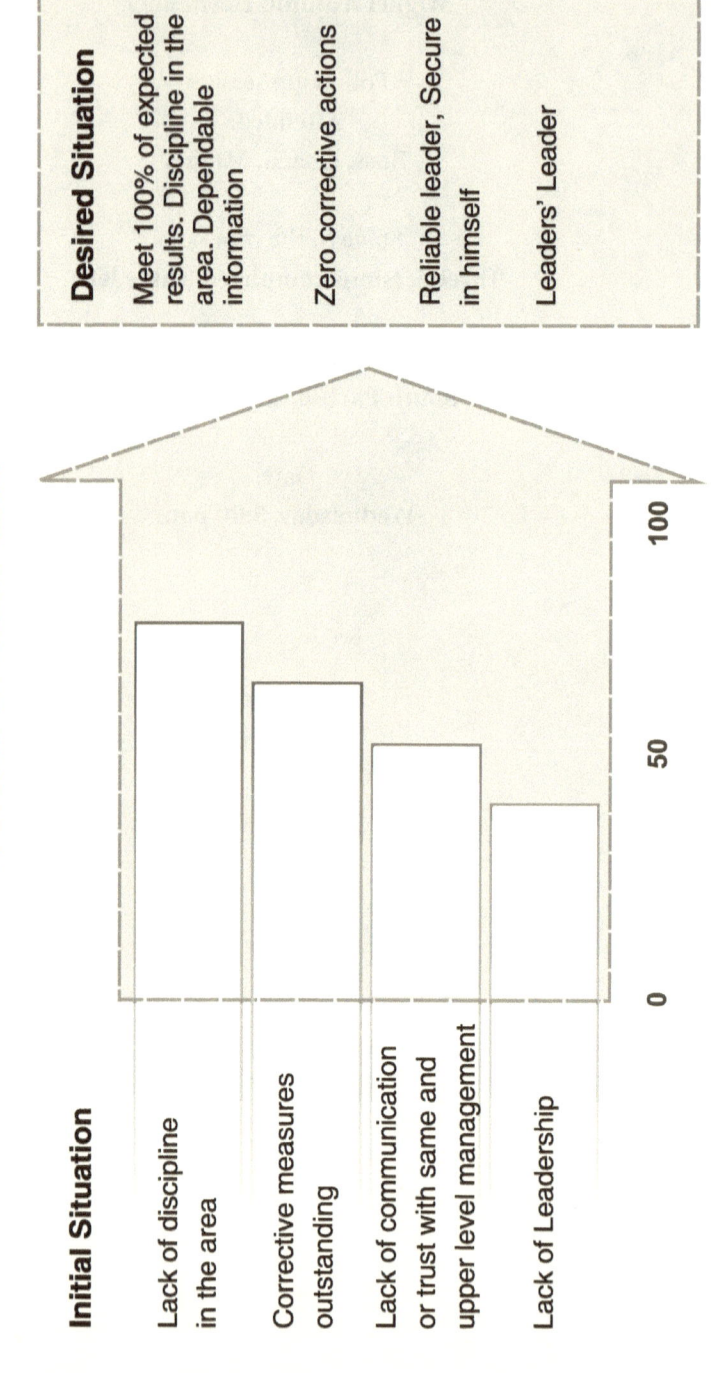

Desired Situation

Meet 100% of expected results. Discipline in the area. Dependable information

Zero corrective actions

Reliable leader, Secure in himself

Leaders' Leader

Initial Situation

Lack of discipline in the area

Corrective measures outstanding

Lack of communication or trust with same and upper level management

Lack of Leadership

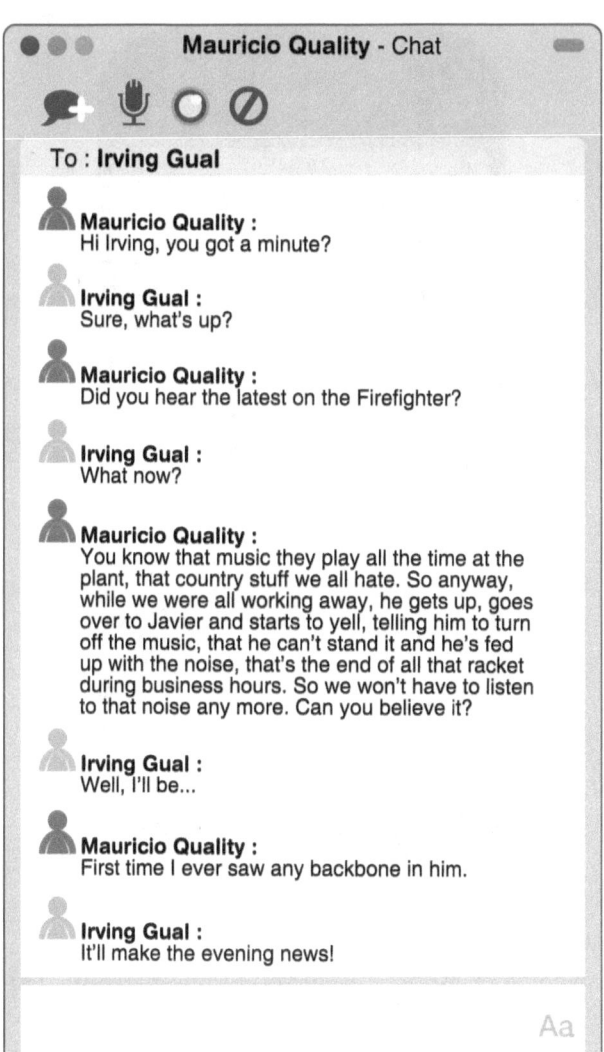

● ● ●   **Mauricio Quality** - Chat   ▬

To : **Irving Gual**

Mauricio Quality :
Hi Irving, you got a minute?

Irving Gual :
Sure, what's up?

Mauricio Quality :
Did you hear the latest on the Firefighter?

Irving Gual :
What now?

Mauricio Quality :
You know that music they play all the time at the plant, that country stuff we all hate. So anyway, while we were all working away, he gets up, goes over to Javier and starts to yell, telling him to turn off the music, that he can't stand it and he's fed up with the noise, that's the end of all that racket during business hours. So we won't have to listen to that noise any more. Can you believe it?

Irving Gual :
Well, I'll be...

Mauricio Quality :
First time I ever saw any backbone in him.

Irving Gual :
It'll make the evening news!

Aa

"Operations manager speaking."

"This is von Stockelsdorf. I wish you a good morning. Do you have a minute?"

"Certainly."

"I'm very impressed; this is the first time in five years that we don't have that noise in the plant. What happened?"

"Looks like Miguel drew a line on it, said the music's got to go and that everyone should focus on their work."

"I thought having noise all the time was the Mexican way of working."

"Well, Miguel ordered it to be turned off for good."

"Good for Miguel. Please congratulate him for me."

"Yes, I'll do that."

"So, good old Miguel is already making some changes?" von Stockelsdorf asked.

"Yes, several. We've already had a follow-up session with the coach, and he seems to be realizing what Teile-X expects from a manager at his level. The Monday meetings have significantly improved and during the daily production meetings, he is following up on issues and demonstrating better leadership of his team."

"Very good. That's the way it should be. That was all. I'm very happy with this peace and quiet."

"Thank you very much."

"Good day."

Chapter 19
The Inner Team Leader

Where there's a team, there's a leader who has the final say in matters. In ordinary terms, this would be the "self" who exerts self-control and is able to speak for us when we deal with others.

Let's imagine Miguel telling his coach how he has found out that the Pleaser is his main protector in *opposition* to the Black Mask, who is *also* acting to protect Miguel while providing a counterbalance to the Pleaser. This all takes place at the first level of consciousness as he descends into the "iceberg" of his inner selves.

As he continues to explore, he discovers deeper voices—more difficult to connect with. It is here that Distressed and the Conformist appear.

On the last level, hidden in the depths, he rouses the Soloist—the one he needs to bring to the surface if he wants to be effective.

The designated team leader needs to coordinate his team and have influence over the different players. Maintaining balance as team leader is subtle and complex, and there are many parts to his job. Among them:

- Taking the conductor's baton to decide whose voice will be heard in each situation, instead of being "possessed" by those voices.
- Maintaining harmony between the inner and external relationships.

- Managing all his inner inhabitants to ensure balance and self-control in difficult situations.
- Holding and facilitating creative "inner team meetings."
- Integration: converting the "mob" into a team of cooperating voices.
- Conflict management: to listen to all polarities. Overreaction can be neutralized by accepting and integrating the disowned selves or voices.
- Taking part in personal and team development and encouraging a spirit of collaboration in each team member.
- Selecting the most suitable players and assigning them a place in the system. Deciding who should be on the field and in what context for a winning game.

Ground Rules

Inner clarity is essential for self-mastery.

The coach's work is of the utmost importance. He helps the client get into the self of his inner team leader. It's important to ask questions and let the leader's voice speak. He is the one who will foster cooperation among the inner selves; the one conferring acceptance of the inner diversity; the one who can listen and moderate and who has clear goals and values from his strategic perspective. Moreover, the team leader needs to have an off-field position, a kind of overall perspective. In this way he stands above what's going on between the voices and acts as a system's manager.

The team leader and the "awareness-generating process"

When he has finished exploring a particular voice, the client needs to physically step out of role, away from the energetic and emotional tension that is part of that self. This is why he is asked to shake it off, to take a few steps, to relax and loosen up his body, and to return to his seat next to the coach where he was before becoming that voice—as we see Miguel do in Chapter 14.

When he gets back to where he was at the start of the session, to where the awareness-generating process occurs, it is important, first, to make sure that the client has "stepped away" from the experience. He can be asked to describe things in the room that he can see, hear, or touch, to know that self to be just a part of him. He will feel himself as physically separated from this sub-personality. Remain silent for a moment to allow him to absorb the experience, and let the awareness-generating process happen. Later on, ask him: "What are you aware of now?" and let him share.

To continue, it is recommended, without being strictly necessary, to give form to the opposing voice using the same technique described above. Start by asking the client to mark a spot in the room for the new player.

After exploring both opposing selves, it is then the turn of the team leader to step in, as is described above. Once the team leader has done his job, the client can start taking ownership of his inner life and becoming accountable for his own results. He will no longer be the same. Transformational learning has occurred for him in the following ways:

- He separates from the one or more selves he had been over-identified with.
- He becomes aware of their polarities, their gifts, and the way they operate in his life.
- He accepts both contradictory selves.
- He discovers the freedom to consciously choose which self to access, depending on the energy and the results he wants in a given situation.
- He uses the awareness-generating process to take responsibility for his inner life.

Chapter 20
The Fall

"I don't understand what you are saying. Tell me, Sister, what's going on!" said Miguel.

"I'm telling you all I know. Please, get down here right away."

"I'm on my way. What happened? They were heading out to buy bread. Who are these animals? What is this place? How did my little brother …?"

Miguel turned on the radio, searching for news. Then, he heard:

"Here is the up-to-date news from Notimex. At this moment, we have two confirmed deaths as a result of a shooting in Apatzingan this afternoon. The first victim is an eight-month-old baby, shot while in the arms of the second victim, his father. He was caught in an exchange of fire between the Michoacan forces of law and order and members of a criminal gang. Sources report that at this time, federal law enforcement has offered support and reinforcements to contain the situation. At least two Black Hawk helicopters are searching the area of Uruapan and Apatzingan."

Miguel turned off the radio. "No, how could this happen?" he said to himself. "Why me? Why us? We're good people; how did we get dragged into it? What can I do? I have to get there immediately. They'll tell me what's going on. They'll tell me it's all a mistake. It can't be true."

How … the little tubby guy … when did I last see him? He was six months old. He was rolling around, trying to get his butt in the air, trying to crawl. He was smiling at everyone. You're not supposed to talk about a baby in the past tense. What's this? This isn't an old man dying! It's Saul's kid. It's my fault. I convinced him to stay in Mexico and try and make it here, instead of getting out like my brothers, who just upped and left. I'm responsible for this. I'll never be able to forgive myself. You have to bite the bullet; now it's down to you. There are only old folks and women left, there's no one else to deal with this. You're to blame, Miguel, he thought.

This was the Black Mask in action.

My own voice is attacking me. I had never realized this before, but this is the voice of truth. Yes, I'm responsible for this. I'm the big mouth; he is the one on a slab. Better if I just shut up for once and for all. Hang on, Saul, I'm coming; I'm on my way. One-way trip to eternity. I could use one of those police helicopters to get there, useless things—they always get there too late to do anything. Collateral damage, they say. This kind of thing doesn't happen to me. It happens on the news. It doesn't happen to us. Why me? Okay, so it happened to my dad's buddy, not too long ago, but not to my family. What am I going to say to Carmen? She's a widow now, and there are no words for someone who has lost a child. What's the name of a childless mother? Widow, if she lost a husband. There is no word for a mother who lost a baby. Forgive me, little brother; I'm to blame for ... for ...

Miguel's cell phone rang. It was his wife.

"What's up?" Miguel asked.

"How are you?"

"As you'd imagine. I'm on the way!"

"They called me. They want to know what time you'll be there."

"What for?"

"It's just that ... no one dares ..." His wife's voice trailed off.

"Dares ... what?"

"To go to the morgue. Maybe you ..."

Miguel was silent.

"Still there?" she asked.

"Yes."

"They're wondering if you ... you all right?"

"Half an hour, tell them."

"Okay."

"Hey ..."

"What?"

"Can you call the company tomorrow? Tell them I'm sick."

"All right."

"And call them on Monday too."

"You've never missed a day's work," she replied.

"Well, it will be my first."

"What should I say?"

"Same thing, that I'm still sick."

From: lennard.stockelsdorf@teile-x.com
To: miguel.hernandez@teile-x.com
CC: Saskia.sussauer@teile-x.com
Subject: Situation

Miguel:

I heard about what happened to your brother last Friday and why you couldn't come to work. I'm sorry for your loss. Please know that you have the unconditional support *of everyone here* at this very difficult time. Take as many days off as you need and *don't worry* about your team. I'm sure they'll get along fine and look after your area so that you can be with your family. *It's the sign* of a good manager that his team can take care of his area when he gets called away.

Saskia, Please arrange leave for Miguel. Let me know if you need anything else.

Mit freundlichen Grüßen/Best Regards
Lennard

From: saskia.sussauer@teilex.com
To: miguel.hernandez@teilex.com
Subject: Support

Miguel:

This is to let you know that the company is offering you bereavement counseling when you get back. This has no connection with your coaching, which will continue as before. Your coach has been told that you'll call when you get back to re-schedule the cancelled sessions.

I'm so sorry that this has happened. I'm with you.

Mit freundlichen Grüßen/Best Regards Saskia

PS: Everyone sends their greetings, especially your guys, who are working very hard so that you don't have to worry about work while you're with your family.

When he got home after a week away, Miguel told his wife, "I found a turtle."

"A turtle?"

"On the road out of Apatzingán. I almost ran it over. And guess what?"

"What?"

"I discovered it's like me."

"How's that?" his wife asked.

"And I've given it a name: Turtle Miguel."

"Yeah … it's got your face," she said, smiling.

"It can run really fast and walk for hundreds of kilometers, but when there's danger, it goes into its shell and stays paralyzed in the middle of the road. It doesn't know it can be crushed. It looks strong, but it's really weak."

"And what does that have to do with you?"

"I'm the same. There's an equally weak Miguel inside me. I've always got this heavy weight on my back; I may be fast, but it's hard on me. I can deal with adversity and it protects me from a lot. If they want to flatten me, they have to hit really hard so I can feel it."

"Feel what?"

"How much it hurts! Here is the turtle that wanders around its turf, as it has always done for hundreds of years. And more."

"More?"

"It doesn't know that the lake dried out in its territory and the new highway was built. It continues on the same old path as if nothing has happened; it can't see the highway," Miguel explained.

"How did you notice it?"

"I was taking my time. Why rush, after all that's happened? I was thinking about what comes next."

"So what does come next?"

"Like the turtle: the next meal, the next sleep, the next step."

"It's huge. How old would you say it is?"

"Around fifteen or twenty."

"Twenty. So, Miguel-turtle," his wife started to ask…

"What?"

"What if you get rid of the shell?"

"I die."

When Miguel went back to work ten days later, he found on his desk something the coach had left for him, with a note saying:

> "I am leaving you this excerpt from a book by Leonardo Boff titled *The Eagle and the Chicken.* I am sharing it with you because I can see the eagle in you; the eagle has recovered its sight and now needs to show its inner strength. Tell me if it's useful; you can write or call me. Big hug, and I hope to see you soon."

> Every point of view is a view from a given point.
>
> —Leonardo Boff

From *"The Eagle and the Chicken"* [10]

In a summer afternoon a goat breeder was coming down from a high plain in the Atlantic forest north of Rio de Janeiro. While he was passing by the foot of the mountain, he came upon a totally shattered eagle nest. Partially covered by twigs, there was a young eagle with a head wound. Covered in blood, it looked dead. It was a rare Brazilian Harpy Eagle, an endangered species.

Picking it up carefully, he thought: "I'll take it to my neighbor, who loves birds and likes to stuff them. Perhaps he'd like to stuff this eaglet."

So he did that. The neighbor felt very sorry for the eagle as he saw it. He also thought it was dead. He gently placed it under a basket.

"I'll stuff it tomorrow," he thought sadly. Next morning he had a big surprise. When he moved the basket, he realized that the eaglet was moving slightly. It had several wounds, it was also blind.

He felt bad for the young eagle. He thought about putting it to sleep. At

---

[10] Boff, Leonardo, *The Eagle and the Chicken. A Metaphor of the Human Condition*

that moment he remembered the teachings of Buddha and Saint Francis. Both of them preached and lived lives of infinite compassion for all suffering beings. He also remembered an ecological principle that states: "Good is everything that preserves and promotes life; bad is everything that diminishes and eliminates life."

With these arguments, he convinced himself not to put down the eagle. He decided to keep it. He started treating it with affection. The eagle, however, was not receptive. It didn't reach out for food or attempt to walk. Without light and without the sun, the eagle was not an eagle.

Every day, the taxidermist would cut up small pieces of meat and keep trying to feed the eagle. After a year, he noticed that its senses were coming back to life. First, its ears twitched – eager when it heard the footsteps that meant food was coming. It would stretch its tail and spread its wings with joy. (An adult eagle, with fully extended wings, can measure more than two meters in length).

Then it started moving on its own. It wandered around the living room and the garden. It perched on a tall tree trunk. Then it recovered its voice, the eagle's typical "kau-kau."

However, it was still blind. For an eagle, eyesight is everything. Their piercing gaze can see eight times more than the human eye. Because it can turn its head 180 degrees, it can see everything that's going on around it.

After some deliberation, the taxidermist decided to put the eagle in with the chickens. An eagle is not a chicken, but a chicken can show it how to live, to move and … who knows? Maybe to inspire a dream of being high in the air and even one day to look for the sun … Who knows?

So the young eagle was brought up with chickens. For two years, it moved blindly among them. Walking was difficult for the eagle; its talons were not made for walking. It would peck here and there, like hens do, but without seeing anything.

So it came to pass one day, the taxidermist realized that a miracle had occurred. The eagle had begun to see. Yes, it could now actually see and identify food with its enormous eyes. After three years of patient care, it had recovered the use of its body. But, having lived with hens, it had become a hen. It ate with the hens, pecked with the hens, and slept in the henhouse.

The taxidermist had long since got used to see the eagle-hen among the rest of the hens, so he stopped thinking about it.

One morning, a stunning couple of great Brazilian eagles flew over the henhouse. They swooped down low to check out the chickens. When the eagle-hen looked up and saw the two eagles, he flapped his wings, shook out his tail started making short leaps upward. He was beginning to know the call of the sun.

After a while, the taxidermist was visited by his friend, the naturalist. They talked about the birds in the region and went out to look at the eagle that had turned into a chicken. The naturalist was mystified by the way the eagle had adapted. Then he announced:

— The eagle will never be a hen. It has the heart of an eagle. That will make it fly. It will again be an eagle, a full eagle.

They decided to try something then and there. They wanted to see how much original eagle was left in the eagle-hen. The taxidermist put a leather guard over his arm. It took some work but they finally managed to get hold of it. The taxidermist placed it on his arm. Urged on by his friend, he spoke to it with a lordly voice:

— Eagle, you shall never stop being an eagle! You've survived so many difficulties! You even got your sight back. You are created to be free and not captive. Stretch out your wings! Soar upward and take your place in the sky!

The eagle seemed bewildered. It didn't move. It looked over at the chickens pecking at their grain, jumped down heavily and joined them.

Encouraged by his friend, the taxidermist did not give up. Next day, he took the eagle from the henhouse. He carried it on the leather guard and climbed upstairs to the roof with his friend. He urged the eagle on with conviction:

— Eagle, you are and forever will be an eagle! Wake up from your dream! Let yourself be who you really are and rise into the sky! Let the sun be born in you! Spread your wings and fly to infinity!

The eagle seemed unmoved by these inspiring words. It looked down and saw the hen pecking at the ground and drinking water from the trough. The taxidermist tossed it upward, hoping it would fly. The eagle flew a meter or two like chickens do and flopped down heavily. He tried once, twice, and a third time. The eagle would not fly. Between the eagle and the chicken the chicken was winning.

The taxidermist remembered the how important the sun was to the sight of an eagle. He asked the naturalist:

— Could seeing the sun help the eagle recover his lost identity?

The naturalist nodded.

Next day, they got up before sunrise. Dawn was magnificent. They went to the rocky summit taking the eagle-hen with them. When they arrived at the peak, the taxidermist held up the eagle and said:

— Eagle, you are friends with mountains and a child of the sun, I beg you: Wake up from your dream! Let your strength be seen! Feel the infinite in your heart! Spread your powerful wings and ascend to the heights!

This time the eagle was paying attention. It seemed to be coming back home after a long absence. It looked around, saw the mountains, and shuddered. As hard as the taxidermist tried to help it by moving it up and down, the eagle could not overcome its fear. The taxidermist couldn't make it fly.

Then for a while he held it firmly in his hands facing the sun. The eagle's eyes began to fill with the orange and yellow hues of the rising sun. In a strong voice, the taxidermist continued to insist:

— Eagle, you have never stopped being an eagle! You belong in the sky and not to the ground! Open your eyes! Drink from the rising sun! Stretch your wings! Fly, eagle!

He held it firmly by its feathered legs, lifted the eagle up and launched it into the air.

It was amazing! The eagle spread his wings out to fill the sky above him, they beat once hesitantly, then a second time with more assurance. It stretched its neck out, its great wings pushing it into the air. It soared into the sky, higher and higher, until it faded into the horizon.

Chapter 21
A View "from the Balcony"

Once we have identified all the different inner voices and spoken to the inner team leader, we need to locate a new "meta position." This is a physical place that represents a perceptual viewpoint, from where the client is able to watch the whole game (which is laid out on the floor with pieces of paper representing the voices/selves). This viewpoint can be from a certain height, standing or even upright on a chair and preferably behind the client.

This position is known as the "view from the balcony." The goal is to help the client take on the role of "Strategic Thinker." It is a position beyond the game itself. It is objective. It creates emotional distance. It allows him to detach from disruptive emotions. In this moment, he can make choices while looking into the future and watching the whole game unfold. It is part of the coaching process for the client to observe himself sitting down there next to his coach, in his role as leader, about to make decisions concerning his inner team.

From this place, the client can see further ahead; he can move forward into the future, and from that point, he can look back at today's confusion and see how he resolved it by changing the lineup of his inner team at the workplace. The Strategic Thinker is a voice that will help him be more conscious and more aware of the whole interconnected network operating within him.

Possible questions for the Strategic Thinker:

- What suggestions do you have for (client), as you look down from this vantage point at various scenarios?
- To reach your goal, which team members will be useful in the situation and which would be better kept on the bench?

Then ask the client to take the pieces of paper with the names of the selves and place them as if they were players on the field (in Miguel's case, the soccer field is his chosen metaphor). Then the Strategic Thinker decides on the best strategy for a winning game. Here, he can swap players around, bring them on as necessary, and plan the moves he would need to deal with different contexts. Go with him to his world and help him see the setting where his new lineup will play. To be sure of achieving his goal, have him describe in maximum detail what the players look like and how they act. If you have the time, it might be interesting to propose some different scenarios and work with the selves themselves, so that step by step, he can assimilate this new way of relating to others and choose the identity (lineup) that will act for him in genuine and effective ways. Help him to feel in his body what it means to have these new scorers. Ask him to visualize himself winning the game.

Chapter 22
From War to Peace

Having overcome his vacillation, jealousy, and insecurity, Miguel, now the battle-scarred veteran, decided to get ready for his hardest fight. He was squaring off against Mauricio, the guy from quality, his rival and main opponent.

During his coaching session, he planned the conversation, the setting, the objectives, and the points that had to be discussed. He paid particular attention to how he was going to stay focused on building agreements that would outweigh the existing personal differences between Mauricio and him. To accomplish this, Miguel, of course, chose the Scoring Soloist to lead his inner team. He knew that the key to successfully managing this difficult exchange was to have the eyes of an eagle and to lead the discussion. This would mean establishing guidelines for the meeting that would prevent either of them from leaving the table before reaching some agreement.

When the day arrived, he got up, looked into the blue sky, took a deep breath, and said out loud, "Today's my day." He felt the confidence of the Soloist, light on his feet and with the long distance vision of an eagle. He was sure the time was right to negotiate and to build.

"Hello, Mauricio," he said when saw his rival coworker. "There's something important I'd like to discuss with you; can I buy you lunch at El Guero? They make great tacos, and it won't be full of people from the plant. We'll have some peace and quiet to talk."

"What's that? Sure, why not. What time?"

"How about 1:00 p.m.?"

"See you there."

When Miguel and Mauricio left the plant, several staff members were amazed to see them together.

***

They ordered their food, and Miguel spoke. "Look, Mauricio, because of everything that's happened in my life over the last few months, I've had the opportunity to think about our professional relationship. Although we both carry a lot of responsibility at the plant, we are locked into a conflict rather than working as members of the same team. This is why I wanted us to meet like this, face to face, and say what we need. I want us both to stay here until we reach some kind of agreement as to how to improve the overall results of our section, which is after all in our interest. If it comes to blows, that's okay, but I refuse to leave the table until we have settled our differences. Tell me if you agree."

"Yeah … okay, go ahead."

"Please tell me everything you disapprove of in the way I work, what you think I should be doing but fail to do, and what you hope we might manage if we were to start with a clean slate.

"Look, Miguel, I can't think of anything off the top of my head. Why don't you start, as it's your idea?"

"All right. I made some notes to keep it all clear in my mind. The first thing I want to know is if you have anything personal against me. Do you dislike me because we come from different social backgrounds, because I didn't have a private-school education, or because I can't speak English perfectly the way you do?"

"What makes you think that? I have nothing against you personally," Mauricio replied.

"Then I don't understand why you keep going for me and putting me down in front of everyone. Tell me if there is anything within my power that I can do so we can act respectfully toward each other. I can't do anything about my spiky hair or my ugly mug, but among the things that bug you, tell me what I can change."

"No … I mean … it's just that you make such a good target. I behave that way with everyone. I'm just joking with you, the way we all do."

"These jokes really affect me. Could you stop making fun of me? Is this something you could commit yourself to?"

"Oh, well, as you're so oversensitive and you take offense at just about anything—"

"This is what I mean; you're doing it right now."

"No, look … it's just that … it's a habit."

"Do you like it when people are disrespectful to you?" Miguel asked.

"Of course not. It's really—in my opinion, I'm just fooling around; it has nothing to do with respect."

"Well, that's what's different about you and me. You see? We have different ways of doing things. To me, these jokes are disrespectful and humiliating. When you say these things, I get enraged and hate you for it. I imagine you see yourself as superior or from a different race … I don't know …"

"I'm sorry, Miguel. I never realized the harm I was doing. I'll do my best to stop."

"You'll do 'your best'?"

"It may be that I'll let some comment slip without noticing …"

"May I point it out to you when you do that, so that you realize it?"

"Please do. Hey, Miguel, I'm really sorry. And I'm also very sorry about your brother—"

"Leave my brother out of this."

"Okay."

"So … do you agree that from now on we show respect to each other, both as individuals, colleagues, and fellow managers?"

"I agree."

"Your words alone aren't enough for me. Maybe I've become too suspicious. Can we put this in writing, as a sign of our commitment?"

"Yes, of course."

"So what are you willing to commit to?"

"To show you respect and not to make fun of you or make unpleasant jokes."

"Thank you. I will make the same commitment," Miguel said while pulling out a notebook and a pen to write everything down.

"Great. Now let's move on to the next item," Miguel continued. "The Monday morning Production meetings are more like a battlefield. You devote yourself to throwing bombs at me so that you come out of it looking like a superstar, and every week, I walk out totally devastated trying to put myself back together. I understand that sometimes we haven't managed to follow up on certain quality findings, but we both know that there are more elegant solutions than waiting for the meeting to humiliate me in front of everyone. Several times, I have asked you ahead of time to let me have the error list in advance, so that I can deal with it in time and avoid being surprised and put to shame by your photos during the meeting. What do you say?"

"Okay, I'll commit to giving you the fault list by Friday afternoon with as many updates as possible, so that you know what's going on and the weekend staff can work on solutions before Monday."

"Sounds good to me. How do you think it will benefit Production?"

"Management will see that we are communicating with each other."

"And the stress our people are under will drop," Miguel added, taking the notebook in his hands. "So what exactly will you commit to?"

"I'll have the list for you by 5:00 p.m. on Friday," Mauricio said.

"My staff will take care of it over the weekend," Miguel added.

"On Monday, we'll talk about the progress we've made."

"I agree. So we're colleagues and coworkers, then?"

"It's a promise."

"So what will happen if you can't deliver on your promises?"

"If for some reason I can't get the list to you Friday, I'll get it to you Sunday night," Mauricio replied.

"And for the meeting, what is your commitment?"

"To announce that we are cooperating with the findings."

"And what about respect?"

"What do you mean?"

"If you break your word?"

"Well, I guess I'll have to apologize … in front of everyone, like the boss did; that took guts."

"Sign here, Mauricio," Miguel said, and they both smiled.

The conversation took a total of four hours. Tacos, desserts, coffee, and one small shot of tequila followed another across the table. There was no point in them returning to the plant that afternoon. Instead, Miguel and Mauricio talked about the need to organize a tour of the plant and jointly inspect problem areas in terms of safety and quality.

They both came up with initiatives to put forward during the management meeting. Later on, they talked about the boss, the director, and their plans for the future and how forging an alliance would increase their effectiveness. They even talked about their families and the possibility of getting their wives and kids together over lunch at Mauricio's ranch half an hour outside the city.

"Thank you, Miguel," Mauricio said, getting ready to leave, while they shook hands firmly. "This is the best conversation I've had in a long time."

"Thank you, too. Let's keep our promises. The truth is that I enjoy peace more than war."

"Can I just tell you something?"

"Sure."

"I see that you have made a lot of changes recently, and I thank you for taking this initiative."

***

The effects of their agreement were immediately noticed. In just a few days, there was a dramatic improvement in their communication, the atmosphere at work became less tense, and the trust level increased.

Miguel and Mauricio started putting forward ideas for the management meeting, they had lunch together, and they were more open with each other. The end of hostilities meant that Miguel's boss was in a better mood, and Miguel realized he was no longer afraid of him. Things in the past that had been insurmountable obstacles became goals that could be met in a calm way.

Miguel had moved pieces within himself, and the whole system moved with him. Miguel became a real manager in what he said and did. Step by step, he was gaining respect.

Chapter 23
Designing Actions

Once the Strategic Thinker has made the necessary changes in the alignment of his inner team, the client goes back to his original seat, where he can assimilate all the polarities, inner dynamics, and selves he has spoken to. He is entering the transformative process and taking his inner life into his own hands. He has separated from some of his selves and has learned to sit between the opposing voices. As part of his awareness-generating process, he will be taking ownership of his voices, listening to their needs, and integrating them. Now it is the time to design his future.

After all these changes in his inner life, the client is not the same person he was when he entered the session. He is much more conscious of what is going on within him. Therefore, the coaching competency "designing actions" will serve him naturally. The coach's job is to help him leave the session sufficiently connected to his own resources to assure the success of his plan.

Possible questions:

- What do you want to do with this particular situation you're working on?
- Which inner self will be representing you now?
- What will you gain from using this voice instead of a different one?
- Now you have this new level of awareness, who are you in this game?
- How will your leadership reflect your awareness of your inner voices?

Another working example of the Strategic Thinker's influence

Situation: Arturo, a coaching client working for a different multinational corporation, went through the process of exploring his selves/inner team members. He had a couple of sessions during which, step by step, he came to grips with the actual role he played in the company and the type of player his bosses were expecting him to be. He discovered, for example, that up to that moment, he had been stuck in the "distant" polarity and his most important need was to find stability or permanence, although his boss was putting pressure on him to become a more active change agent. The more the boss pushed, the more resistant Arturo was. If such dynamics had continued the way they were at the beginning of the coaching process, it's quite possible that Arturo would have left the company.

After several sessions, he finally got an understanding of what the whole game was about, as well as the benefits and risks of his position. When he went to the last position, that of the Strategic Thinker "from the balcony," he saw that he had been over-identified with a self that was not helping him in his job. He also discovered his personal metaphor and could create a strategy that would help his career.

In order to understand this strategy, let's take another look at the model of the Riemann-Thomann polarities:

The following four players in the image correspond to the chess moves that Arturo needs to have on each board in this model:

1. The queen's game, to move effectively between change and closeness.
2. The bishop's game, to play well on the change and distance board.
3. The knight's game, to create closeness and stability.
4. The king's game, to maintain distance and stability.

The Queen's Game

Change

Time

Space

Closeness

The queen's game: to move effectively between change and closeness

Description	Flexible, adaptable, entitled to protection
How does she move?	Offers alternatives for change. Proposes and finds connections between moves or events that are apparently unconnected or seem unimportant
How does she relate to others?	The queen is open, trusting.
How does she make decisions?	In the short term, because any move can change the game
What's her goal?	To win in a situation that is unstable and risky. The queen wants to live.
What does she need the most?	To move and to always have support: she needs others. She needs partnership, dialogue, closeness with her team.
What is her main fear?	To lose. To be left alone without protection
When does she lose?	When she doesn't consider her protectors, whatever their rank, and ends up alone. (And when she fails to pay attention and anticipate the other side's moves)
What's her strategy?	To collaborate, build alliances and meaningful multidimensional relationships. To acknowledge everyone's point of view. No one is belittled or looked down upon.
What's her language like; how does she speak; what are her keywords?	Openness, looks for options, optimistic, collaborative, communicates directly and openly. Does not allow the environment to affect her. There's always an opponent, but she concentrates on the best way of setting up her game while watching what the other is up to. Talks in present tense, but thinks about the future and the best game layout
What should I get rid of to play the queen's game?	The need for permanence and distance, expectations, "shoulds," and having to be right

The Bishop's Game

Change

Time Management

Space Management

Distance

The bishop's game: to play well on the change and distance board

Description	Entrepreneur. Makes independent decisions, but not without taking others into account
How does he move?	Proposes changes or ideas more independently, in light of his experience, while considering the opinions of others. Self-starter, but seeks support when necessary. Can go all the way to the other end of the board if it's part of his strategy
How does he relate to others?	Negotiator. Appears and disappears. This way, he can provoke uncertainty in his opponent.
How does he make decisions?	In the medium term, and keeps reviewing alternatives
What's his goal?	To win, individually and with his team
What does he need the most?	To be independent but supported by his team. To get closer when necessary for him or the team. And to walk away if in danger. To protect his kings
What is his main fear?	To lose, individually and with his team. To lose his independence
When does he lose?	When he does not develop projects independently and when his team or team members become disorganized
What's his strategy?	To develop projects, to get things started, to train his team. To enter or exit the situation as necessary
What's his language like; how does she speak; what are the bishop's keywords?	Innovations, comradeship, independence, direct communication, team and opinion. To get in-volved or walk away as necessary
What must I get rid of to be able to play the bishop's game?	Habits and routines in whatever way you can. From believing that being remote is the only way. You often need to get closer.

The Knight's Game

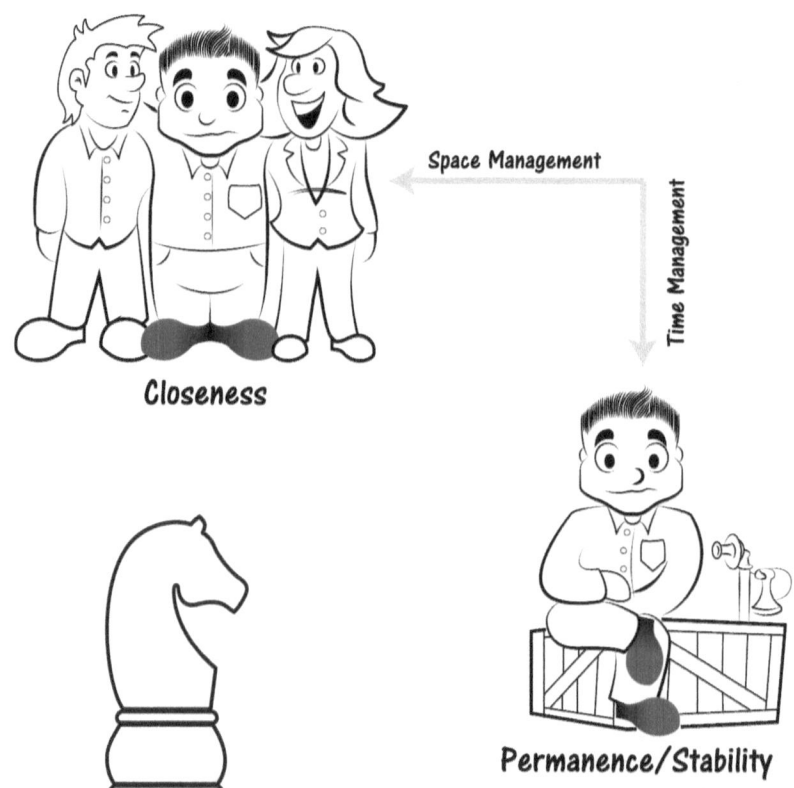

Closeness

Space Management

Time Management

Permanence/Stability

The knight's game: to create closeness and stability

Description	Moves and jumps really well, able to adapt to minor changes. In intimate communication with the rest of the players
How does he move?	Jumps over the heads of others. In constant communication to follow up on changes, when the changes are made he continues in the same direction. He will change his game in coordination with others and backed by personal experience. Seeks constant support
How does he relate to others?	Agreements, relationship. By surprising them
How does he make decisions?	Short and medium-term. Does his work and follows the opinion of the team
What's his goal?	To be a key piece in the winning strategy. In many games, he is the piece needed to guarantee checkmate.
What does he need the most?	Teamwork, support, constant communication, to be on good terms with his higher-ups
What's his main fear?	Flaws in the relationship between him and his team. Moving around the board in a senseless way
When does he lose?	When he loses touch with his team; when he no longer reflects the consensus and starts acting on his own
What's his strategy?	To develop partnerships, more in the planning than at the action stage. To build relationships with working groups
What's his language like; what are the knight's key words?	Talks about relationships, communication, closeness, mutual reliance. His key word is *team.*
What should I get rid of to play the knight's game?	Individualism, silence, not sharing

The King's Game

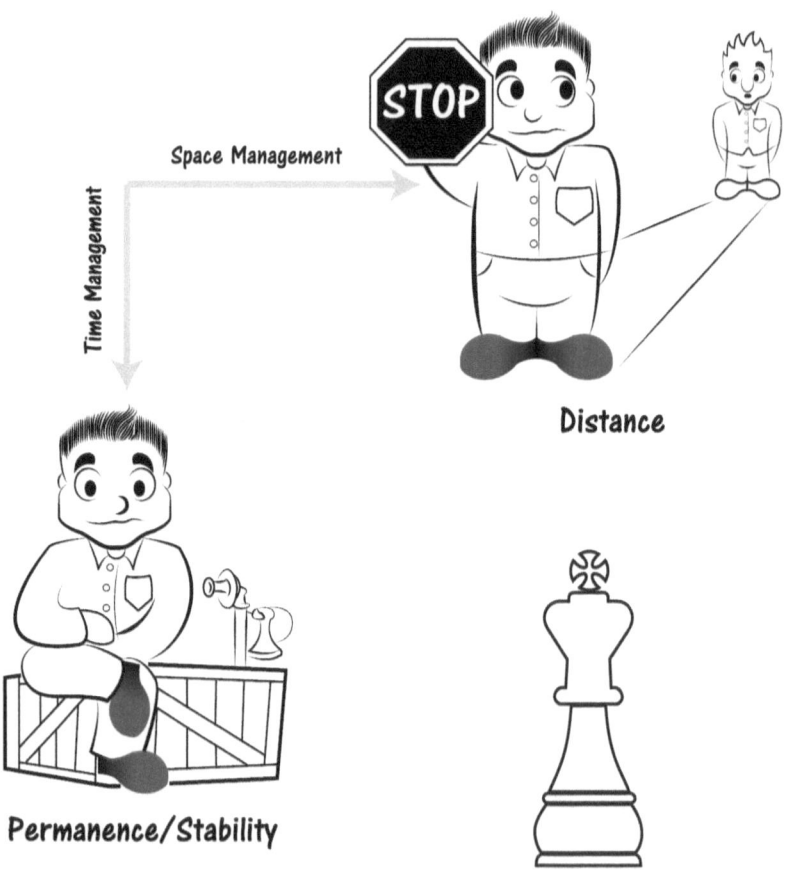

Space Management

Time Management

Distance

Permanence/Stability

The king's game: to maintain distance and stability

Description	Stable. Doesn't change his mind. Inflexible. Independent
How does he move?	Makes decisions independently. Needs to communicate. Hardly changes. Hardly moves. Seeks support when needed
How does he relate to others?	He's the king. He has no need to move. The other pieces are there to take risks and give their lives for him. He is lonely. Others protect him.
How does he make decisions?	Medium- and long-term. Holds true to his original course. Takes very few risks
What's his goal?	To stay on the throne. To be protected by his attendants
What does he need the most?	His stability, his independence, and his experience. Unconditional fidelity and loyalty from his subjects
What's his main fear?	Improvisation, instability, change, being close to the enemy. Finding himself unprotected and not knowing what to do
When does he lose?	When he no longer communicates with his most loyal subjects. When the queen abandons him. When most of his protectors are dead and he is helpless before the enemy.
What's his strategy?	Strategy based on tradition, values, and unconditional loyalty in relationships. Trusting in the abilities and vision of his own team
What's his language like; what are the king's key words?	Independence, consistency, stability, long-standing relationships. Loyalty. Upholding tradition
What should I get rid of to play the king's game?	Lack of trust. The belief that "I'm independent and don't need anyone else."

Why was it useful for Arturo to assemble this strategy? So that he could free himself from his original unbending ways and embrace flexibility without feeling threatened. He realized that if he wanted to be effective with those on opposite poles to himself, he would have to move "with a different piece." In other words, it would be necessary to adapt his game and his way of dealing with the different selves. Additionally, he would need to line up his players in support of his actions and understand in what way the energy of each player could best help him succeed.

The above example demonstrates the importance of securing a strategic view first, so as to be able to select the type of game and the players to put on the board. Then, the detailed work is carried out in step-by-step planning. Some of the actions might include having conversations with key individuals, making certain decisions, preparing complex meetings, or whatever else the client finds he needs to do to step out of his comfort zone. It is necessary to confirm that the actions planned at each step are legitimate and reflect the aim, the strategy, and—above all—the identity of the client. Who does he want to be in this game?

Chapter 24
The Results

"Hello."

"Is this the coach?" a female voice asked.

"Yes. Who's speaking, please?"

"This is Miguel's wife."

"Miguel's wife? Oh, I'm honored. How can I help you?"

"He doesn't know I'm calling you. I took your number from his phone list."

"Is there anything wrong?" the coach asked.

"It's just that I want to thank you."

"Thank me?"

"Yes. Look, I don't know if the coaching is working for his job or not, but what I can tell you is that ever since he started working with you ... this was before ... what happened to my brother-in-law and his son ... before all that, he'd become like someone else here at home."

"Someone else?"

"Yes. I feel that you got me my husband back, the Miguel I got married to. Since he started with the coaching ... he's different."

"So, tell me please, what is different about him?"

"Everything. In the past, he'd just say yes to everything, but he wouldn't do anything except stay hooked to his smartphone fixing problems at the plant until midnight. He'd hardly talk at all. He'd turn on the TV and wouldn't even spend time with the children. He was moody all day long and would complain loudly, but without saying anything. Well, he didn't even look at me, you know. I could've dyed my hair blue, and he wouldn't have noticed a thing."

"So … how is he now?"

"He's getting home early for the first time in his life. He's turning off his phone before dinner and says that his team needs to learn to deal with any issues that come up. He plays with the kids. He takes the guitar and sings to them. He's here, you know? I mean, in body and soul. The truth is that he hasn't told me anything about what goes on during the sessions with you, but when he has a session, he comes back in better shape than before. This is why, truly, I thank you with all my heart."

"Thank you very much. I really appreciate your calling me and I hope every day gets better."

"I want to ask you a favor: don't tell him I called you. Let this stay just between you and me."

"Very well. I won't tell him anything."

Final Report
Coaching of
Miguel Hernández Pérez

General objectives:

To become a leaders' leader; to achieve this, he needed to improve the following points, which were low in his initial evaluation:

- To make sure, by managing his team, that everyone is working toward the same objective.
- To effectively coordinate activities between his and others' areas.
- To be able to prioritize his workload.

- To stay calm and confident even under pressure and when facing difficult-looking situations.
- To talk openly and transparently about issues.
- To balance daily activities with a long-term vision.
- To anticipate and facilitate the resolution of conflicts.
- To motivate people to work as a team.

1. Initial situation: conditions at the start of the process

When I got to the first session, I felt severely burdened and under huge pressure from work. I wondered if I could deal with the commitment, if I would fail, and if I was the right person for the position. I didn't trust myself or others. What is more, I felt that the environment was hostile and that I was a victim of the situation. I felt that I couldn't build a team with anyone, that things were getting so complicated that I was going to go under. I felt very lonely with all these difficulties. I wanted to take care of everything but solved nothing.

In general terms, I was facing the following:

- Absence of a problem-solving approach.
- A high level of personal stress caused by thinking that everyone was against me.
- A lack of confidence in others (poor communication, especially with peers and my boss).
- Absence of teamwork.
- Attempting everything and resolving nothing.

2. Desired situation: the goal he wanted to achieve

First of all, to know where I was and where I wanted to go, and to have a clearer picture of my role in the organization. An important objective was to take ownership of my role as manager and how I saw my career in the company. To think about the responsibility I faced, not only knowing that I had the right profile for my current position, but also able to look forward in time and see the changes I would need to make to reach the level of manufacturing manager.

Among the specific objectives I set for this process were:

- To create a procedure for reviewing information and making plans.
- To follow up with and execute plans.
- To involve all team members.
- To improve communication, especially with coworkers at my level and with bosses.
- To encourage commitment and engagement.
- To underline the benefits for individuals who want to move forward and take responsibility.
- To fulfill, maintain, and create new commitments, personally, with other managers, and with my boss.
- One of my most important objectives was to recognize opportunities to develop my leadership style and change them.

3. What changed during the coaching; what did you discover as you went through the process? What measurable progress did you make?

I succeeded in getting closer to my peers and started building alliances with those I needed in order to reach my goals.

I started noticing that I was meeting with others, not to help them reach their goals, but for them to help me achieve mine.

I became more disciplined. I have been learning to be consistent in order to maintain results, and I am more assured in what I do and what I say.

If I have doubts, I only have to look at how working as a team can lighten the workload.

I realized that collaboration with others was the way out of my original dilemma. In so doing, I was the one who stood to gain the most—both personally and professionally. The best example of this was my relationship with Mauricio—which had more conflict in it than any other. Now we collaborate and work as a team.

It was important to change how I perceived myself within the company. I understood that I wouldn't be able to do anything by myself. I understood my role. I had to change my attitude, I had to contribute more of myself and my resources; this meant getting closer, being open, and trusting others.

This was crucial. I had to understand and make it understood that we all need to work toward a common end, that we're all on the same side and that things will get better just by improving the working atmosphere.

4. Results

- Performance is better. I have systematically promoted follow-up of action plans and processes, although there are still some opportunities for progress.
- It was like a cascade: first building and then working as a team with the right information to hand, then asking for what I need. I act as a filter. We establish priorities, and based on these, we can see where best to invest our resources and effort, because I have a better view of what is going on.
- Feeling empowered as a manager.
- A clearer vision of myself, my position, my potential, and my future in Teile-x.
- A change in perspective from believing that I was all alone carrying the world on my back and overloaded with problems, to seeing myself as a competent, effective manager who makes decisions and assumes responsibility for his results.
- A focus on achieving objectives in an efficient and consistent manner. Basically, to know that we need to work as a team.
- Coordination of our activities and improvement of the work environment. My relationship with the rest of the managers and my boss has changed substantially. Thanks to this, it is a lot easier to agree on things, to work together and to do what is best for production.
- Dealing with the personal issues that were in the way of my effectiveness and growth.

5. Added value: How much value did this add to my personal and professional effectiveness?

- Now I feel a lot more confident with the team. I feel that the environment supports me more in demonstrating my abilities, ideas, and suggestion; the things that I used to keep to myself because of my mistrust.

- Trust has significantly improved our teamwork. By giving myself the space to make mistakes instead of getting lost in the idea that if I failed I'd lose my value as a person, I realize it's the opposite. Now if something goes wrong, I just make an extra effort and pay attention that it doesn't happen again.
- The value of learning. To keep in mind how, to start with, I was unaware of my incompetence. Now I work at developing my competences so they become habits.
- The value of discovering my own capabilities.
- I have learned that if I want to, I can work with another person, even if that person is difficult.
- I have learned what it means, in concrete terms, to not just be a leader, but a leaders' leader.

6. Goals and objectives beyond the coaching process

- To maintain the structure and procedure for resolving inherent problems within the system that have no easy solution. Always invite the participation of areas that can help me solve problems and support a culture of problem-solving. To stop thinking I can fix everything on my own.
- To get closer to and speak more with my boss, about planning as well as our daily work objectives.
- To feel surer of myself when I make decisions.
- To keep going with my stress management.
- To continue learning on a constant basis in order and acquire all the leadership skills a leaders' leader should have.
- To ensure I walk the talk. If I ask others to be open, I must also be open. That's my commitment: to be consistent.

Presentation of final results

In the same meeting room where Miguel, the plant manager, the Human Resources manager, the boss, and the coach met at the beginning of the process.

"Well, Miguel, so now we are at the end of what we started," von Stockelsdorf said. "How quickly six months have passed. First of all, I want to tell you how grateful I am that you put a stop to that music from the loudspeakers. I know I told you at the time, and I can now see how this was tied in with your coaching. Now I can work in peace, and I think that we have all greatly benefited. Anyway, enough of that. I've seen other changes in you, but first of all, let's hear what you have to say. I am interested in seeing your presentation."

Miguel smiled and stood up. Calmly and without fear, he went and stood next to the image that was projected on the screen, showing the same chart he had created for the follow-up session. Just like a soloist before starting to sing, he took a deep breath, looked at each one present, and said, "The written document I have just submitted contains a complete description of the process, as well as the lessons learned. For the presentation, I believe this chart I have created will be enough. In it, I summarize all that this coaching process has meant for me. As you will see, none of the four bars has achieved 100 percent, because I believe I still have more to learn."

"I like the fact you haven't given yourself a hundred; it shows that you are self-critical and can improve more." Stockelsdorf interrupted. I like this clear and concrete chart. As a German, I don't trust it when someone gets one hundred for everything. If you have one hundred, then there's no opportunity for improvement, and all of us can improve, as we are not perfect— though we are perfectionists. But go ahead, please. Sorry I interrupted."

Miguel spoke for ten minutes. At the end, he thanked everyone and asked for their feedback.

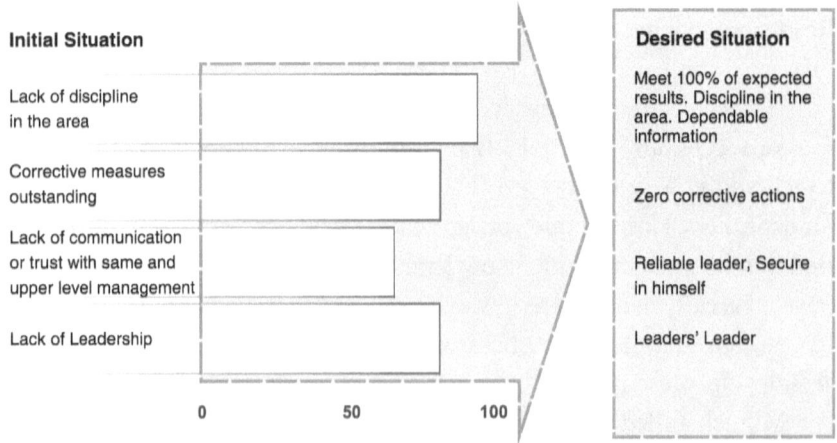

Miguel Hernandez Coaching Follow-up

*Objective :
- To become the leaders' leader

Initial Situation

Lack of discipline in the area

Corrective measures outstanding

Lack of communication or trust with same and upper level management

Lack of Leadership

0   50   100

Desired Situation

Meet 100% of expected results. Discipline in the area. Dependable information

Zero corrective actions

Reliable leader, Secure in himself

Leaders' Leader

Von Stockelsdorf spoke first.

"I can say what I have observed in you. In the meetings, I've seen a Miguel different from the one I used to know. Now I see that when you stand up, everyone looks at you. And you remind me of my own coaching, because it was there that I, too, learned to stand before an audience and speak. Now I say, 'this is a manager' when you answer back with correct and accurate information. Now I believe you have control over your area, and I see discipline that reflects order and the 5S "[11]. Very good, Miguel. I am happy with your results. You know you have my support when you need it, although you also have your boss and I don't intend to jump the queue. Please send me this presentation. I don't need any other reports."

Then, Stockelsdorf looked at Miguel's boss and asked, "Do you have anything to say? What changes have you witnessed in Miguel?"

"I must be very sincere. At the beginning of the process, I had my

---

[11] 5S is the name of a workplace organization method that uses a list of five Japanese words: *seiri, seiton, seiso, seiketsu,* and *shitsuke.* The list describes how to organize a work space for efficiency and effectiveness by identifying and storing the items used, maintaining the area and items, and sustaining the new order. There are five 5S phases: They can be translated from the Japanese as "sort", "straighten", "shine", "standardize", and "sustain". (Wikipedia)

doubts as to whether Miguel was the right person for the position we wanted to promote him to. I was about to give up. Now that some time has passed, I can see that much has changed. I have to recognize that I've learned a lot from you, Miguel, and that I admire the way you have stepped into the bullring with this challenge. In spite of the terrible things that happened to your brother, you didn't give in, and you moved on, probably even stronger. Today, I can see that the production area is much better coordinated. Now I see you all working as a team, with more respect and collaboration. I hope we continue with this close relationship and that every time you need something, you come to me, and I hope above all that everything you've been building will be maintained over time." He stopped and looked at the coach. "I don't know what you did, but having started this process, something else has popped up. Okay, now ... how did you say you're doing with your English, Miguel?"

"That's a priority now. I haven't missed a single class in the last month."

"You're touching on a good point," said von Stockelsdorf. "I was wondering how I could help you with your English, and I got an idea. You could look after our corporate guests when they come. I'm assigning you the job of taking them to lunch and dinner in order to put your English to work. As neither I, nor your boss will be there, you will be forced to practice. Agreed? This way you will be seen by them and they will get to know you. So over to you, coach. Is there something you want to say?"

"Well, that it's time to hand over. The coaching stage is over, and now you will be responsible for the follow-up and sustainability of results, so that Miguel can continue to evolve and become a leaders' leader. I am honored to have had the privilege of walking the path with you, Miguel. You're an extraordinary human being, and I'm certain that you will be able to face any challenge required by the company. Now I see that you have a clearer vision of who you are, what you are capable of doing, what you want, and how you need to relate to both your team and the rest of the organization, in order to be the most effective leader that you can be."

Looking at the boss and von Stockelsdorf, she added, "I thank you for trusting Miguel's potential and for having backed his development so that he could discover the leader living inside him and take command. It's clear that it's not a matter of creating a fairy tale where 'everyone lived happily ever after.' That's not real life. Right now, Miguel, we're here because you took the fundamental steps to become the person you want to be. You must keep in mind that you'll always encounter obstacles, enemies, and internal demons. You will face and defeat them, provided it's clear in your mind who you are and who you want to be in each one of the circumstances that you confront in life. Lastly, I'd like to recall something we talked about during a session, something that is applicable to all of us: whatever we do, wherever we are, let's allow ourselves to enjoy it. Can you imagine how this company would be if you were all consciously focused on giving the best of yourselves just because you're happy working here?"

Five months after completing the coaching process, Miguel wrote to his coach to report that he had been selected for a position in the United States. He was so happy!

Final Thoughts

The more I apply the inner team model to my coaching practice, the more convinced I am on its transformational learning. I have successfully implemented it with the most diverse clients, some of whom were managers in similar situations to Miguel. I have used it with individuals from Europe, South America, Asia, Africa, and Mexico, with housewives, psychologists, university professors, government officials, and professional coaches.

The inner team model offers the client an accessible way of visualizing himself in order to discover obstacles within himself that limit his effectiveness in life.

At the beginning of the process, some clients can't see that well how their behavior impacts others. Their eyes and ears can only see and hear the outward reality. Their use of language is aimed at talking about others or saying too much. This makes it more difficult for them to get in touch with their inner life. It's as though they need to take some initial steps to develop their consciousness so that they can then connect with their inner selves and there discover the origin of their conflicts with the outer world. For this type of client, the inner team model has been very successful. It's just a matter of timing and the readiness of each person.

Working with this methodology is especially useful for the client who wants to learn how to manage his emotional life and to stop being prisoner of his mind and slave of his impulses. Discovering that some feelings are the voice of an "inner self" and having this voice talk to the client, as if it were another person, is a powerful resource—widely used in similar disciplines. By doing so, the client can dis-identify or dissociate himself from it and embrace the fact that it is just one of the many selves that inhabit his inner life. In other words, becoming aware of the fact that he is much more than just one of his inner voices, he can decide where to place each of them, in what kind of game they will be most useful, and when it would be better to keep them waiting on the bench.

"I had never thought about this;" "This is something deep;" "This is new to me;" "I didn't know that I had this inner voice living within;" "I never realized I had a voice inside that tells me things;" "For the first time in my life, I see that it's possible to do something to handle my anger/shyness/anxiety;" "I had never talked about this before;" and "I feel relieved and lighter now just knowing that this self is out there and that I can call him if I want" are just a few of the many ways in which clients describe their surprise and the impact it has when they get in touch with their inner team.

Working with the inner team is closely linked to the communication model that I translated from German, *Das Kommunikationsquadrat*, as "the Schulz Quartet." It provides a four-directional tool for inquiry that guarantees complete communication of an event, a goal, or a self.

The ultimate origin of our inner selves is fear. Nobody wants to feel fragile or vulnerable, and we create a comprehensive system of protection that shields us from the threat of not meeting our basic needs. As the client gains access to his inner team, he starts discovering those things that were wisely hidden under the behaviors that were not very effective and led to a polarized state. When he dares to lift the first layer and take a "peek," he is opening a door of transformational learning that will give him more integrity in his relationships.

For the coach, the challenge is to start working with his own inner life—his fears and his systems of protection. Without this, he would be blind to his client's inner life. Other approaches or methodologies may require the coach to "keep his distance" from what happens with his client; this cannot be done when working with the inner team. It requires a deep commitment to oneself.

It's important to know how powerful this model is: it is effective from the moment it's first used.

The more powerful the tool is, the more care must be taken when using it. Before deciding to work with it, you need to make sure that you yourself have experienced what it means to separate from your inner voices and to embrace your own polarities, so that you know how to handle them. You need to set your ego apart and acknowledge your own vulnerability. The coach must assume the responsibility involved in working with a client and his or her inner team. The methodology has to be respected. It's not like a recipe. This is a deep and serious approach to helping human beings find a more conscious way of relating to themselves, to the roles they play, and to other people.

Once you have tried for real, you will find it's addictive. There's no way back.

Which scenarios are open now?

Mastering the use of the inner team model can only happen if the coach dares to delve within himself and discover the connections among the seemingly separate parts. In life, everything is connected and part of the whole. It is not possible to "erase" or "forget" the nature of an inner voice, as they tend to appear through the "back door" the first time we stop paying attention. (We don't want to experience what Tom Cruise's character went through in the film *Magnolia*. This is a clear case of someone who was the prisoner of voices that he persisted in denying.) Working with this model means going through the process of reunification, reintegration, and alignment of numerous inner parts that seem to operate as if they belong to a divided brain.

The coach also needs to pay attention to the connections between himself and the client, the ones he has with his social context, with events in the Middle East or climatic change. Events that happened centuries ago on another continent might shed some light on our current behavior. Everything is related to everything else, even if inconveniently so. Systems theory, molecular biology, and quantum physics have been providing scientific evidence on these matters for some time already. But this knowledge of a world in which each part and each being is connected to the whole and affects it is thousands of years old. This idea is found in documents dating from 2,500 years ago.

In my experience, I have discovered that as a principle, these connections go from general to particular; they move from the surface to depth; they change from being loud and noisy to silent and subtle. They are able to dissolve the external human mask to show its true loving self. The connections, finally, enable us to transform ourselves from warriors into Conscious Leaders.

The deeper you get, the greater awareness and connection you experience. This means exploring increasingly hidden layers in order to reach higher levels of consciousness. What is certain is that the more a person acts from his or her center, the more fulfilled his or her life becomes.

As a voice being nourished by countless voices, the voice of coaching needs to keep on growing and strengthening the human systems in which it is developing. There is an important area of research that is helping to advance our understanding of the art, science, and practice of professional coaching.

We still need to research the underlying realities that are hidden under/behind our behavior. We are called to learn from the wisdom of ancient cultures instead of trying to reinvent the wheel. The ancient cultures still offer enormous gifts to us if we have the vision and clarity to learn from their lessons, instead of only searching for "new" approaches that in the end … are not new at all.

One of the temptations I fell prey to was the search for learning. For many years I had been moved by an inner seeker, who was insatiable, searching for more and more trainings, workshops and certifications. There never seemed to be enough until I realized that the issue had nothing to do with learning and trying more and more approaches but rather with delving deeper and deeper into my selves. The longer I have been in the process of owning my disowned selves and experiencing this continuous awareness-generating process, the more I have found "true north." It is not that the Seeker has vanished, no. I'm just keeping things in balance. I know, too, that there is no such thing as an ultimate source of satisfaction, pleasure, effectiveness, knowledge, or happiness. As I become my mind's owner and liberate it from my inner prisons, then I know that this journey through inner landscapes, voices, contradictions, selves, devils, monsters, and fairies is worth it.

The scenario that is revealing itself to me now is as broad and vast as the history of humankind.

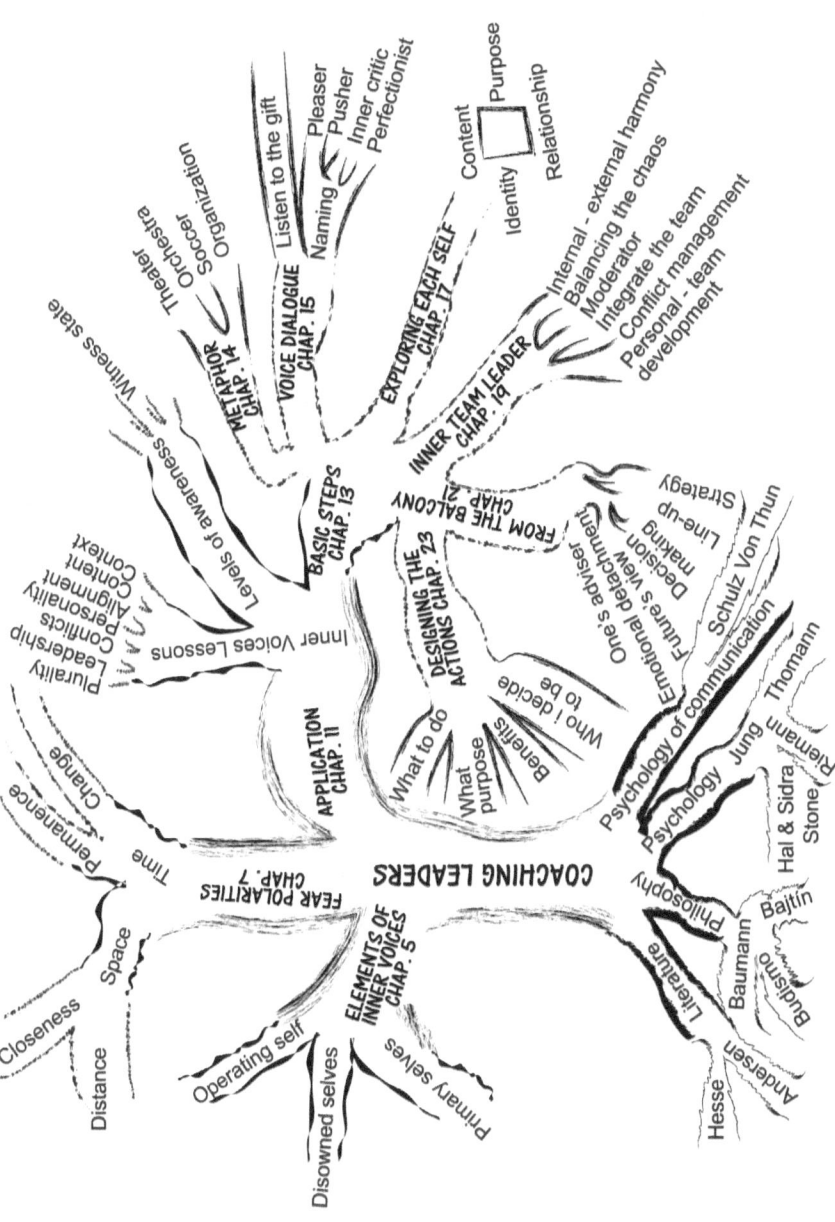

Bibliography

Alejos García, José: "Identidad y alteridad en Bajtín," Acta Poética, 27 (1) Primavera. Universidad Nacional Autonoma de Mexico, 2006.

Andersen, Hans Christian: *Fairy Tales from Hans Christian Andersen.* Russel Ash and Bernard Higton (eds.), Chronicle Books, 1992.

Bajtín, Mijaíl: Yo también soy. Fragmentos sobre el otro. Editorial Taurus, Mexico, 2000.

Bajtín, Mijaíl: Estética de la creación verbal. Siglo XXI Editores, Mexico, 2011.

Bauman, Zygmunt: Liquid Modernity. Polity Press. 2000.

Boff, Leonardo. *The Eagle and the Chicken. A Metaphor of the Human Condition.* 1999.

Bojorquez, Mario: "Fernando Pessoa: el hombre multitudinario". *Círculo de poesía,* Revista electrónica deliteratura. Septiembre de 2009.

Bubnova, Tatiana: "Voz, sentido y diálogo en Bajtín." Acta Poética 27, Primavera. Universidad Nacional Autónoma de Mexico, 2006.

Erhard, Werner: *The Heart of the Matter.* San Francisco (set of 3 audiocassettes), 1984.

Fischer-Epe, Maren: Coaching: Miteinander Ziele erreichen. Rohwolt Verlag. Hamburg, 2007.

Hesse, Hermann: *Steppenwolf.* Alianza Editorial, Mexico, 1998.

Riemann, Fritz: Grundformen der Angst. Eine Tyfenpsychologische Studie. Reinhardt Verlag, Munich, Basel 1989.

Schulz von Thun, Friedemann: Das innere Team in Aktion. Rohwolt Sachbuch, Hamburgo, 2004.

Schulz von Thun, Friedemann: Miteinander reden 3: Das innere Team und Situationsgerechte Kommunikation. Rohwolt Verlag, Hamburgo, 2005.

Schulz von Thun, Friedemann: Miteinander reden: Kommunikationspsychologie für Führungs- kräfte. Rohwolt Taschenbuch, Hamburgo, 2007.

Stone, Hal and Sidra: *Embracing your Inner Critic: Turning Self Criticism into a Creative Asset.* Harper San Francisco Editions, San Francisco, 1991.

Stone, Hal and Sidra: *Voice dialogue basic elements: Relationship and the Psychology of Selves.* Nataraj Publishing, California, 2007.

Stone, Hal and Sidra: *Embracing Heaven and Earth: a Personal Odyssey.* Delos, Inc. Albion, California, 2009.

Vygotsky, Lev: *Thought and Language. Massachusets Institute of Technology, 1987*

Wertsch, James: Voces de la mente. Paidos, Buenos Aires, 1993.

Contact Laura at:

www.sistemahagakure.com

laura@sistemahagakure.com